STARFINDER

Development Lead • Robert G. McCreary
Authors • Amanda Hamon Kunz, Thurston Hillman, Jason Keeley, and Owen K.C. Stephens
Cover Artist • David Alvarez
Interior Artists • Leonardo Borazio, Victor Manuel Leza Moreno, David Melvin, Mirco Paganessi, and Pixoloid Studios (Aleksandr Dochkin, Gaspar Gombos, David Metzger, Mark Molnar, and Ferenc Nothof)
Cartographer • Damien Mammoliti

Creative Directors • James Jacobs, Sarah E. Robinson, and James L. Sutter
Director of Game Design • Jason Bulmahn
Managing Developer • Adam Daigle
Development Coordinator • Amanda Hamon Kunz
Organized Play Lead Developer • John Compton
Developers • Crystal Frasier, Jason Keeley, Joe Pasini, and Linda Zayas-Palmer
Starfinder Creative Lead • Robert G. McCreary
Starfinder Design Lead • Owen K.C. Stephens
Starfinder Society Developer • Thurston Hillman
Senior Designer • Stephen Radney-MacFarland
Designers • Logan Bonner and Mark Seifter
Managing Editor • Judy Bauer
Senior Editor • Christopher Carey
Editors • Lyz Liddell, Adrian Ng, and Lacy Pellazar
Art Director • Sonja Morris
Senior Graphic Designers • Emily Crowell and Adam Vick
Franchise Manager • Mark Moreland
Project Manager • Gabriel Waluconis

Publisher • Erik Mona
Paizo CEO • Lisa Stevens
Chief Operations Officer • Jeffrey Alvarez
Chief Financial Officer • John Parrish
Chief Technical Officer • Vic Wertz
Director of Sales • Pierce Watters
Sales Associate • Cosmo Eisele
Vice President of Marketing & Licensing • Jim Butler
Marketing Director • Jenny Bendel
Outreach Coordinator • Dan Tharp
Director of Licensing • Michael Kenway
Organized Play Manager • Tonya Woldridge
Accountant • Christopher Caldwell
Data Entry Clerk • B. Scott Keim
Director of Technology • Dean Ludwig
Senior Software Developer • Gary Teter
Community & Digital Content Director • Chris Lambertz
Webstore Coordinator • Rick Kunz

Customer Service Team • Sharaya Copas, Katina Davis, Sara Marie, and Diego Valdez
Warehouse Team • Laura Wilkes Carey, Will Chase, Mika Hawkins, Heather Payne, Jeff Strand, and Kevin Underwood
Website Team • Robert Brandenburg, Lissa Guillet, Erik Keith, and Eric Miller

ON THE COVER

Eox may be a dead planet, but its surface still harbors dangers to both the living and the undead, such as the jiang-shi vampire Captain Zeera Vesh featured in this volume's cover art by David Alvarez.

PART 3 OF 6

SPLINTERED WORLDS

This book refers to several other Starfinder products, yet these additional supplements are not required to make use of this book. Readers interested in references to Starfinder hardcovers can find the complete rules of these books available online for free at **paizo.com/sfrd**.

Paizo Inc.
7120 185th Ave NE, Ste 120
Redmond, WA 98052-0577
paizo.com

Printed in China.

SPLINTERED WORLDS

ADVANCEMENT TRACK

"Splintered Worlds" is designed for four characters.

5 The PCs begin this adventure at 5th level.

6 The PCs should reach 6th level before heading to Eox in Part 3.

7 The PCs should be 7th level by the end of the adventure.

ADVENTURE BACKGROUND

Centuries ago, an evil and malicious elven mystic named Nyara lived a depraved existence on Castrovel. At the time, the Cult of the Devourer was merely a shadow of a threat to the civilized species of the galaxy, but Nyara discovered in the dogma of the Star-Eater the nihilistic ambition for which she later became known. Nyara fed off the pain and suffering of those weaker than her, and she slaughtered hundreds and quickly rose through the ranks of Castrovel's Star-Eater cult. As the number of atrocities she committed in the Devourer's name mounted, Nyara came to believe that her uncaring patron would visit a terrible fate on her soul should she not work to further the total destruction of existence that the Devourer so coveted.

Committing herself fully to the Devourer's entropic cause, Nyara began a career in dark soothsaying. Her killings became ritualistic rather than indiscriminate, and she drew prophecies from the very blood of her victims. Nyara spent her long elven life span extracting the terrible secrets underlying creation and extrapolating innumerable doomsday futures. Before her death, Nyara recorded her most profane divinations in her magnum opus, a tome called *The Entropy of Existence and Glorious Rise of the Void*. This work, though obscure to the galaxy at large, is considered a key unholy text to many Devourer cults. Its dark prophecies span countless realities, including dozens of ways that the multiverse and all its planes of existence might someday come to an end. But Nyara transcribed her predictions in imprecise and enigmatic language, as prophets are wont to do, and the scattered Devourer cults have had little success in parsing the elven mystic's words and bringing her prophecies to fruition.

Until, that is, a Devourer cult recently looted an archaeological site on Castrovel called the Temple of the Twelve. Inside this ancient observatory and temple, the cult discovered documents describing a celestial body named the Gate of Twelve Suns and its possible connection to an alien superweapon called the Stellar Degenerator. The Castrovel cult transmitted these findings to a parent cult, headquartered in a secret asteroid based called the Star-Eater's Spine in a treacherous sector of the Diaspora known as the Field of the Lost.

Upon receiving the information found in the Temple of the Twelve, the Diaspora cult had an astonishing revelation: one of the cryptic divinations in *The Entropy of Existence and Glorious Rise of the Void* foretold the appearance of a vastly powerful weapon from beyond time and space that would first lead to the destruction of several star systems and then to the destabilization of existence itself. Combining these two sources, the Devourer cult now believes that Nyara's prophecy refers to the Stellar Degenerator and suspects that the Gate of Twelve Suns is the key to finding the demiplane that houses the alien weapon. The cult still does not know the exact location of the Gate of Twelve Suns, but Nyara's oracular writings provided one more clue: an obscure reference to a distant star system called Nejeor. Convinced that the means to finding the Gate of Twelve Suns lies in the Nejeor system, the Devourer cultists hastily erased the data they received from Castrovel and set out for Nejeor, abandoning their asteroid base in the Diaspora.

Meanwhile, the exiled Corpse Fleet of Eox has been monitoring the activities of a group of Starfinders from Absalom Station who explored both the derelict ship *Acreon* (which was carrying a Corpse Fleet officer as "cargo") and the asteroid called the Drift Rock (which the Cult of the Devourer believes is a fragment of the Stellar Degenerator). When the Starfinders clashed with the Cult of the Devourer at the Temple of the Twelve on Castrovel, the Corpse Fleet was able to trace the Castrovel cult back to its parent cult in the Diaspora. Curious about the cult's interest in the Starfinders and their discoveries, the Corpse Fleet dispatched a ship to the Diaspora, arriving at the Star-Eater's Spine just days after the cultists abandoned the asteroid base for Nejeor. In short order, the Corpse Fleet's savvy undead hackers restored the cult's deleted files, learning about both the existence of the Stellar Degenerator and the cult's destination in the Nejeor system. Obsessed with the idea of gaining control of the alien superweapon for themselves, the Corpse Fleet again erased the cult's files and set off in pursuit.

The race is on to find the Gate of Twelve Suns and seize control of the Stellar Degenerator, and the Cult of the Devourer and the Corpse Fleet are already steps ahead of the Starfinder Society. The doomsday clock ticks ever toward midnight, and if no heroes step forward to thwart the cult and the undead navy, the end may come sooner than even the malefic prophet Nyara might have hoped.

As the adventure begins, the PCs should be aware that the Cult of the Devourer is actively searching for the Gate of Twelve Suns and the Stellar Degenerator—an ancient alien superweapon that would devastate the Pact Worlds (and countless other star systems) if it fell into the cult's hands. Although the PCs likely defeated Tahomen and his Castrovelian cult cell at the end of "Temple of the Twelve," they also learned that the cult leader shared his discovery with another Devourer cult in the Diaspora. The adventure assumes that the PCs are dedicated to stopping the Cult of the Devourer from finding the Stellar Degenerator; indeed, the PCs might already be planning to head to the Diaspora to search for the Devourer cult base and determine what these dangerous cultists are plotting to do with the information they've learned, as well as to find out what else the cultists know about the Stellar Degenerator, given its dire capabilities. The PCs can stop off at Absalom Station along the way to purchase supplies or upgrade their gear, provided they don't linger on the station too long.

If the PCs don't get in touch with their Starfinder associate **Chiskisk** (N host shirren) on their own, the shirren contacts them to learn the results of their expedition to Castrovel. If the PCs are uninterested in following the lead from Castrovel to the Diaspora, or if they seem unaware of the urgency surrounding this mission, Chiskisk attempts to impress the gravity of the situation upon the PCs. Chiskisk's signature refined enthusiasm transforms into anxiety and near panic at the prospect of the Cult of the Devourer finding a weapon like the Stellar Degenerator, and with alarm, the shirren encourages the PCs to find the cult's base in the Diaspora so the Starfinder Society can determine just how much information the cult has and how its members might be planning to act on it. If nothing else, Chiskisk points out that if the PCs can find the Gate of Twelve Suns and the Stellar Degenerator first, such a major discovery would be an achievement of historical proportions, for both the PCs and the Starfinder Society. In any case, Chiskisk requests that the PCs keep them regularly informed of their progress.

Finally, given the situation's dangerous nature, Chiskisk offers to reward the PCs for their efforts. If the PCs can track down the Cult of the Devourer in the Diaspora, the shirren promises a payment of at least 2,000 credits to each PC—and possibly more, if the Starfinder Society can find sponsorship from additional parties concerned about the cult's threat.

Regardless of whether the PCs undertake this mission on their own or at Chiskisk's behest, the PCs still have their work cut out for them. On Castrovel, the PCs were able to determine only the approximate location of the Devourer cult's base in the Diaspora: somewhere in a treacherous stretch of several hundred asteroids known as the Field of the Lost. Fortunately, a reliable Drift beacon floats just outside this region of the asteroid belt, but without an exact location, the PCs must search the Field of the Lost for clues to find the Devourer cult base there.

EVENT 1: A RUDE WELCOME (CR 6)

The journey to the Diaspora is not detailed in this adventure and should be largely uneventful. Arriving at the Field of the Lost, a bleak sight greets the PCs through their starship's viewscreen: irregular chunks of rock and ice and occasional ominous fields of green and blue floating through an empty void, with a vast field of stars for a backdrop.

Give the PCs a few moments to get their bearings, and then ask the PC who is acting as the starship's science officer (or captain, if no PC is serving as science officer) to attempt a DC 16 Computers check. On a success, the PC notices a few peculiar blips on the starship's instrument panels that indicate irregular movement in the PCs' vicinity—another ship lurks nearby! The PCs can go to their battle stations to engage in starship combat. If the PCs fail to detect the other ship, they learn they're under attack when the enemy ship opens fire on them.

Starship Combat: The space pirates called the Free Captains operate throughout the Diaspora, and while their base, the asteroid known as Broken Rock, is located thousands of miles away, the pirates nonetheless recognize that the remote and relatively hostile Field of the Lost represents an undefended back door into their territory. As a result, in recent decades the Free Captains have ensured that at least one of their number regularly patrols the Field of the Lost for pirate hunters or other intruders looking to establish a foothold in the Diaspora that might threaten Broken Rock.

Currently, the job of patrolling the Field of the Lost has fallen to Alera Okwana, the ambitious human captain of the pirate vessel *Rusty Rivet*, which has noticed the PCs' presence in the area and is preparing to launch a stealthy attack against them. Captain Okwana aims to make her name keeping meddling nonpirates from lingering in this treacherous stretch of space. The *Rusty Rivet* has been making rounds through the Field of the Lost for several weeks, and things have been mostly quiet except for the recent arrival—and subsequent quick departure—of a Corpse Fleet ship. Captain Okwana did not engage the ship, believing it could easily overwhelm the *Rusty Rivet*, so she settled for lurking nearby and watching where it went. She likes her odds against the PCs' ship better, however.

This encounter uses the starship combat rules beginning on page 316 of the *Starfinder Core Rulebook*. If the PCs did not detect the *Rusty Rivet*'s presence, the pirate ship gets to act in a free gunnery phase (meaning the pirates can shoot at the PCs but the PCs can't shoot back, much like how a surprise round works in tactical combat). Otherwise, the starship combat occurs as normal.

The *Rusty Rivet* is a Nebulor Outfitters Starhopper; the ship's stat block is printed on the inside front cover of this volume. A PC can identify the make and model of the *Rusty Rivet* with a successful DC 11 Engineering check to identify technology. A PC who succeeds at a DC 15 Culture check can recognize the ship's affiliation with the Free Captains of the Diaspora (see page 476 of the *Starfinder Core Rulebook* for more information on this organization).

If the PCs want to avoid combat, they can try to hail the other ship and convince its captain not to attack with either a successful DC 26 Diplomacy check to change attitude or a successful DC 25 Intimidate check to bully. In this case, Captain Okwana invites the PCs to her ship for a parley, as described in The Rusty Rivet on page 5. If the PCs fail either check, the *Rusty Rivet* attacks.

RUSTY RIVET — TIER 4

Nebulor Outfitters Starhopper (see inside front cover)
HP 65

Development: Although the *Rusty Rivet* begins this starship battle aggressively, Alera Okwana is more ambitious than bloodthirsty. If the PCs reduce the *Rusty Rivet* to fewer than half its Hull Points, Captain Okwana uses her ship's comm unit to hail the PCs. If the PCs respond, Okwana offers to surrender and talk with the PCs. If the PCs don't respond or refuse to accept Okwana's surrender, the *Rusty Rivet* fights until it's disabled (at 0 Hull Points), at which point Okwana transmits her surrender again. See The Rusty Rivet below for details on the PCs' interactions with the pirate crew.

Story Award: If the PCs defeat the *Rusty Rivet* in starship combat, award them 2,400 XP for the encounter.

The Rusty Rivet (CR 6)

Once the PCs have shown that they won't be easy prey for the *Rusty Rivet*, either through diplomacy, intimidation, or skill in combat, the savvy Captain Okwana recognizes that she has been bested. She powers down her weapons and hails the PCs, promising that her crew will put up no resistance if the PCs board her ship to discuss terms.

If needed, a map of the *Rusty Rivet* is presented on the inside back cover of this volume.

Creatures: The *Rusty Rivet*'s crew consists of Captain Alera Okwana, engineer **Q4** (NE male android), gunner **Korrina "Steel-Fang" Noh** (N female korasha lashunta), and pilot **Zekanoya Spikesmasher** (CN male vesk). As the PCs board the pirate ship, the crew follows their captain's orders and assumes nonthreatening poses.

This encounter is open-ended, and its results depend on the PCs' decisions during roleplaying, but it is not intended to be a combat encounter. The adventure assumes that the PCs defeated the pirates in starship combat; there is no need to defeat them a second time in personal combat. Should combat break out between the PCs and the pirates, however, see Development on page 6.

Captain Alera Okwana is surprisingly cheerful and cheeky for a surrendering pirate, though her quick wit and practical banter cover a coldly calculating mind that's constantly assessing the best way for her and her crew to survive this encounter. Captain Okwana is bold and ambitious, but she is also a savvy survivalist. She cares about her crew, but she has little personal investment in her mission or ship beyond how both might help further her goals— to make a name for herself as a Free Captain and build a decent fortune before retiring to a more peaceful spot in the galaxy.

As soon as it becomes clear that the PCs are willing to talk, the ever-practical Okwana readily admits to her status as a Free Captain, explains her assignment to patrol the Field of the Lost and guard against threats to the Free Captains, and makes it clear that—as long as the PCs aren't coming after Broken Rock—she has no disagreement with them personally. Attacking the PCs' ship was all just a misunderstanding, Okwana says with a wide grin. The pirate captain spends as much time talking with the PCs as they wish. Her responses to some of the PCs' likely questions are as follows.

Why did you attack us?/What do you want? "We're pirates! Isn't it obvious? Though to be true, I'm a Free Captain. Still green, but I'm not too big to admit that, now, am I? The senior captains say the best way to prove myself is to float around this dump for a bit, fight off any pirate hunters, and capture

ALERA OKWANA

loot for the home rock. But you're not here looking to muscle in on the Free Captains, are ya? So let's be done here, and we can each go on our merry way, yeah?"

Have you encountered any other starships out here? "Not much, to be true. No Steward-backed antipirate armadas, no fat merchant freighters; just a few sarcesians here and there. And a couple of nasty-looking bone ships. Big bruisers, and frankly above my pay grade, ya know? But they didn't care about us little old pirates, so we just shadowed 'em for a bit. They did whatever business they had here and went on their way."

(If the PCs press Okwana on this point, or ask whether the ships were Eoxian, she simply smirks and shrugs. She doesn't know much about Eox or the Corpse Fleet, or why they were interested in the Field of the Lost. However, a PC who succeeds at a DC 20 Culture check recognizes Okwana's description of the "bone ships" as being consistent with those commonly associated with both Eox and the Corpse Fleet.)

What was the bone ships' business here? "How should I know? They flew around, landed on a few rocks, and left. Not my problem anymore."

Do you know anything about the Cult of the Devourer or any sort of cult base nearby? "Yeah, there are cultists out here. Crazy buggers—I suggest giving 'em a wide berth if you come across any. They got a hole on a nearby rock where they get together and do whatever it is cultists do. They call it the Star-Eater's Spine, or something equally stupid. Come to think of it, those bone ships were headed in that direction."

Where is the Star-Eater's Spine? "We think the rock they hole up on is one we call K9204. I've never been there, so I don't know if there's a base there or not, but I can point you in the right direction." Captain Okwana punches some commands into the *Rusty Rivet*'s computer and brings up a navigational chart of the region, which she copies onto a datastick for the PCs. The chart shows the route to Asteroid K9204 (area **A**).

So where do we go from here? "Way I see it, you beat us and got us dead to rights. I admit that. But there's no reason we can't be friendly-like. I'll give ya 1,000 credits apiece to let us and the *Rivet* go. You go your way, we go ours. Everybody's happy and nobody dies, yeah?"

If the PCs press the issue, a successful DC 16 Diplomacy check to change her attitude or a successful DC 25 Intimidate check prompts Okwana to increase the offer to 1,200 credits apiece. (Threats of violence might prompt the pirates to attack, however; see Development below.)

ALERA OKWANA — CR 4

XP 1,200

Female human soldier

N Medium humanoid (human)

Init +9; Perception +10

DEFENSE — **HP** 47

EAC 16; **KAC** 18

Fort +6; **Ref** +4; **Will** +5

OFFENSE

Speed 25 ft.

Melee carbon steel curve blade +9 (1d10+5 S; critical bleed 1d6)

Ranged thunderstrike sonic rifle +12 (1d10+4 So; critical deafen [DC 15]) or frag grenade II +9 (explode [15 ft., 2d6 P, DC 13])

Offensive Abilities fighting style (hit-and-run)

TACTICS

During Combat Although she has surrendered, Captain Okwana is a crafty survivalist who fights dirty if it means surviving to see another day. If combat breaks out, she remains mobile, trying to spread out her ranged attacks among as many foes as possible. If enemies are spaced far apart, Captain Okwana moves into melee combat with her curve blade against those she's already hit from range.

Morale If Captain Okwana is the only surviving pirate, she again tries to surrender. If her offer is refused, she fights grimly to the death.

STATISTICS

Str +1; **Dex** +5; **Con** +3; **Int** +0; **Wis** +2; **Cha** +2

Feats Opening Volley

Skills Computers +10, Intimidate +15, Piloting +10, Stealth +10

Languages Common, Sarcesian

Gear officer ceremonial plate, carbon steel curve blade, thunderstrike sonic rifle with 2 high-capacity batteries (40 charges each), frag grenades II (2)

RUSTY RIVET'S CREW (3) — CR 1

XP 400 each

Space pirate crew member (*Starfinder: First Contact* 15)

HP 20 each

Development: If the PCs make overt physical threats against Captain Okwana or her crew, there is a chance that the pirates rethink their surrender and decide to attack the PCs. Each time a PC makes such a threat, there is a 20% chance that the pirates believe they must defend themselves with force. What constitutes a physical threat is ultimately up to the GM, but actions such as brandishing a weapon or stating violent intentions are prime examples. If any PC outright attacks a pirate, combat starts immediately. If the PCs required the pirates to surrender their weapons at the beginning of the encounter, Okwana retrieves a frag grenade she's hidden in a nearby compartment and throws it at the PCs to distract them, while her crew each spend 1 round accessing hidden caches of weapons to rearm themselves and attack the PCs.

If the PCs kill Captain Okwana and her crew without learning about Asteroid K9204 and its location, they can still find the information on the *Rusty Rivet*'s computer. A successful DC 21 Computers check to hack the system allows the PCs to access the pirate ship's tier 2 computer, where they can find the navigational chart that identifies Asteroid K9204 as a base for the Cult of the Devourer called the Star-Eater's Spine. The pirates' data is incomplete, however, as the Free Captains are unaware that the Star-Eater's Spine (area **B**) is actually a subterranean base inside Asteroid K9204 (area **A**).

Story Award: If the PCs talk with Captain Okwana and learn about Asteroid K9204 and the Devourer cult's base from her, award them 1,600 XP. If the PCs fight and defeat the pirates in tactical combat, award the PCs XP as normal, but they gain no additional story award for learning about the cult's base.

A. Asteroid K9204

The information from the *Rusty Rivet* points the PCs to a small asteroid not far from the site of their engagement with the space pirates. It takes the PCs 1d4 hours to navigate their ship through the Field of Lost to the planetoid. Officially designated K9204, the asteroid is less than a mile in diameter and is made up of treacherous rock- and ore-infused terrain. Jagged cliffs cover the asteroid's surface; in fact, there's only one relatively open area of any size on the entire asteroid. The asteroid is dense enough to provide low gravity (*Starfinder Core Rulebook* 402) and is enveloped with a thin atmosphere (*Core Rulebook* 396).

Unless otherwise stated, the large expanses of rock depicted on the map on page 8 take the form of sheer cliffs that rise about 40 feet high and stabilize into flat surfaces. Collected in the crevices at the base of the cliffs—as well as at the bases of the smaller rock formations—are drifts of a strange sort of space ash made up of metal flakes, rocky grit, and space dust. This ash is the product of a disastrous decades-old mining venture that ground the asteroid's rock and ore into dust.

There's only one open area on the asteroid large enough to accommodate a starship, located immediately east of the area depicted on the map. Deep grooves and scorch marks in the rocky ground show that starships have landed and taken off from this area repeatedly, though no such ships are currently present. Once the PCs land, they can head to either area **A1** or **A5**. The Devourer cult base is nowhere in sight; the PCs must explore the asteroid's sole navigable area to find the secret door that leads to the cultists' underground base (see area **A3**).

A1. Sniper's Cove (CR 5)

This narrow pass is flanked by a sheer rocky wall to the north and a more slender—though just as tall—rock formation to the south. A deep pile of silvery ash sits in the cleft between the cliff and a stepped outcropping. Otherwise, the rugged ground is pockmarked but flat.

This area affords the easiest access to the top of the asteroid's cliffs 40 feet above. In the area's northeastern extremity, the sloping rock has been carved into steps leading to the formation's pinnacle, and similar natural steps exist along the outcropping shown in the area's northwest corner. The rocky steps up to the cliff are each about 3 feet high (and can provide partial cover) and are considered difficult terrain. Similarly, the cliff is irregular enough that a creature standing on top of it has cover against attacks from the base. From the cliff top, creatures can see across most of the asteroid's surface, which is covered in treacherous cliffs

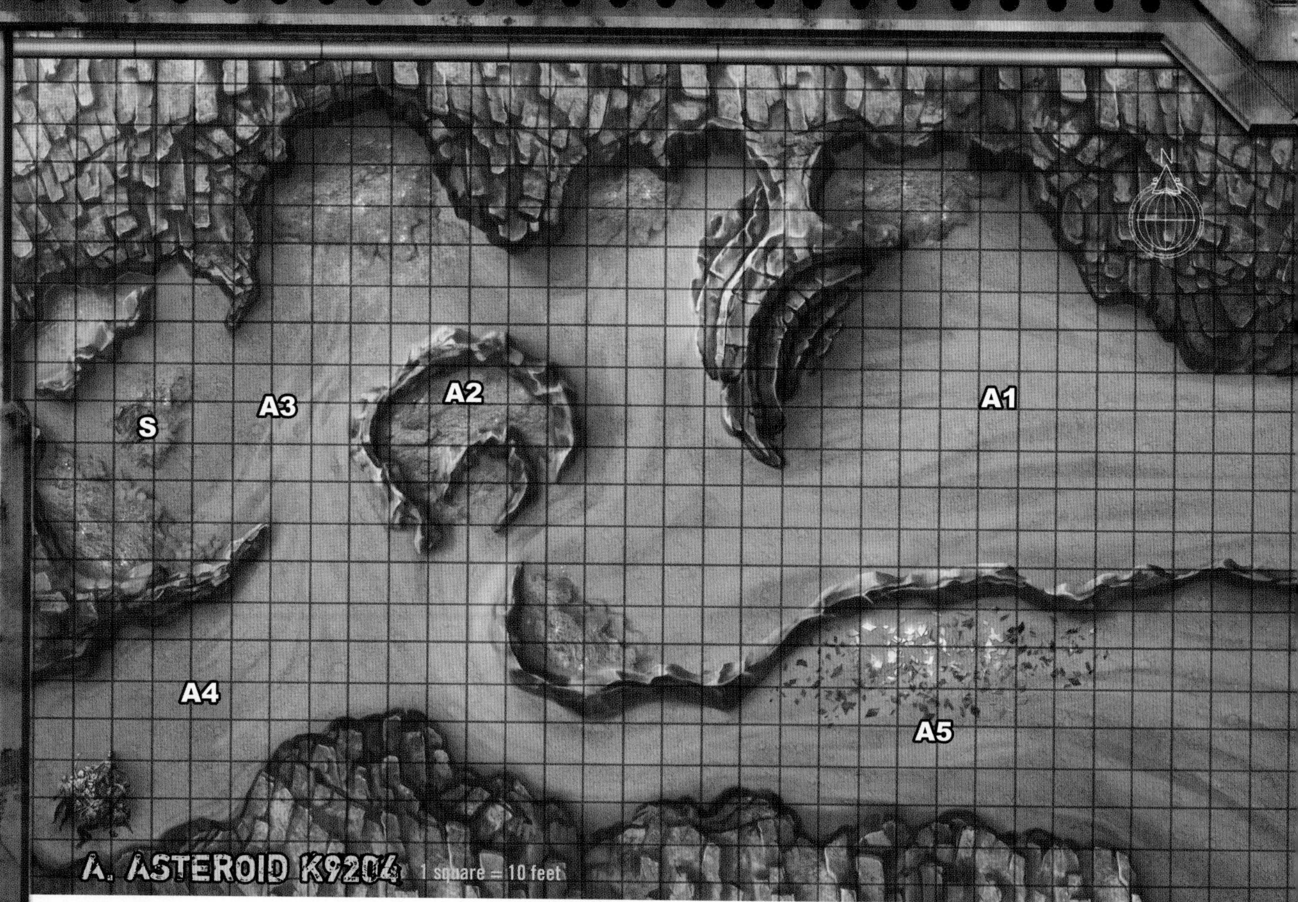

and rock formations. It's obvious that this area is the only one that affords access to the asteroid's rocky surface; its other areas are not traversable.

Creature: Lurking on the top of the cliff to the north is a sarcesian sniper named Yex. A few weeks ago, Yex meandered to this asteroid to escape the overbearing politics of his home, a nearby and much larger planetoid. Having brought a month's worth of provisions, Yex thought this isolated asteroid valley was the perfect getaway. However, he soon fell under the mental influence of the skreesire in area **A3**. Now, Yex is firmly under the skreesire's command and has been convinced to defend this area against intruders with his life.

Yex immediately notices the PCs enter this area and positions himself at the edge of the cliff, using Stealth to hide behind cover. After a few rounds of observation, he makes a ranged attack against a random PC he can see with his sniper rifle, seeking cover afterward for sniping again.

YEX CR 5

XP 1,600

Male sarcesian sniper (*Starfinder Alien Archive* 98)

HP 64; **RP** 4

TACTICS

During Combat Yex uses Stealth to make sniping attacks from the top of the cliff while keeping his position hidden. If opponents climb the cliff to confront him, Yex runs down the nearest stairway to avoid his attackers and shoot at them from below.

Morale Yex is fully convinced that he must kill any creatures that disturb this part of the asteroid. Under the skreesire's influence, the sarcesian sniper fights to the death.

Treasure: Sifting through the 5-foot-deep silvery pile of ash in the crevice between the rocky outcropping and the cliff reveals the presence of a months-old humanoid corpse dressed in tattered black and red rags. A successful DC 10 Life Science check reveals that the corpse was once a human, and a successful DC 15 Mysticism check identifies the iconography on the corpse's clothing as symbols of the Devourer. There is little of value on the corpse that isn't rotted, but on one of its bony fingers is a filthy *ring of sustenance*.

In addition, a PC who succeeds at DC 18 Perception check while on top of the cliff finds a small, cloth-wrapped bundle stashed in a crevice. Inside this bundle is a mobile hotelier with a drained battery, six R2Es, a credstick loaded with 2,800 credits, and a small leather-bound journal.

The journal belongs to Yex, and perusing it reveals a couple of months' worth of handwritten entries in Sarcesian (characters who don't speak Sarcesian can translate the journal with a successful DC 25 Culture check to decipher writing). The entries describe the stubborn sarcesian's disagreements and personality clashes with others of his kind on his nearby home, and they detail his decision to leave and spend a month cooling down on this asteroid. The journal entries become increasingly jumbled going forward. References to a "flesh beast" recur multiple times until Yex begins referring to this same creature as "master."

Maudlin praise of the creature as a higher power suddenly gives way to gibberish written in no known language. The journal's final entry simply reads, "Yex keep scratchies away so master finally make Yex into skree YES." This sentence might seem nonsensical, but a PC who succeeds at a DC 20 Life Science check recognizes it as a possible reference to a skreesire, a creature known for controlling the minds of its enemies (and which can be found in area **A3**).

A2. Skreeling Hive (CR 6)

Thin rock formations here curve almost elegantly to form the rough shapes of caves and tunnels, with piles of silvery ash nestled against them like snow drifts.

The ash piled against the rock faces is much more uneven than elsewhere on the asteroid, ranging from a foot deep to 4 or 5 feet deep. All squares with ash in them are considered difficult terrain.

Creatures: This cave-like area is home to a lurking trio of skreelings that feed on the silvery ash. Those skreelings that live long enough and eat enough ash eventually grow into skreesires (see area **A3**). The skreelings lair inside the enclosed chamber formed by the rock walls near the center of this area, where they have gathered and stored drifts of ash. When they detect approaching intruders (such as the PCs), the skreelings use Stealth to hide behind rocky formations (although the skreelings can fly, the top of the formations are too narrow for them to find a foothold, so they hide on the ground). When a PC moves adjacent to a hidden skreeling, the creatures burst out of hiding to attack the PCs in a surprise round.

SKREELINGS (3) CR 3

XP 800 each

HP 35 each (see page 56)

TACTICS

During Combat The skreelings try to flank opponents as much as possible, attacking with their claws and taking advantage of their cluster ability.

Morale The PCs have intruded upon the skreelings' territory and interrupted their feeding, and they are therefore threats the creatures can't ignore. The skreelings fight to the death to try to drive the intruders away.

Treasure: Although Yex (the sarcesian sniper in area **A1**) didn't know it, a couple of sarcesians from his home planetoid recently traveled here to check on him. The sarcesians knew of Yex's affinity for holing up in small, secluded spaces, so they entered this cave complex in search of their friend, only to run afoul of the skreelings. The ravenous creatures made quick work of their victims, and the sarcesians' bodies now lie in the ash heaps abutting this area's southernmost rock formation. The dead sarcesians still have some of their gear, and aside from their torn-up and useless armor, two advanced Diasporan rifles (*Starfinder Alien Archive* 99), two tactical dueling swords, and two credsticks holding 1,500 credits apiece can still be salvaged.

The ash filling the two northern alcoves in this area mostly covers old bones. However, if the PCs spend 10 minutes digging through the ash in the northwest corner, they find a partially intact skeleton in a sitting position. The skeleton's armor and flesh have long rotted away, but across its lap is a thin, jagged, and rusted piece of metal. Emblazoned on it, in Castrovelian, are the barely legible words "Imura Excavations." A PC who succeeds at a DC 18 Perception check notices four bars of pure silver ore behind the skeleton's back, worth a total of 4,800 credits. The skeleton and silver are remnants of the failed mining expedition to this asteroid decades ago that ended with disastrously macabre results, and they are not directly tied to this adventure's plot.

A3. Skreesire's Lair (CR 7)

This isolated grotto is dotted with piles of silvery ash. To the northwest, a low shelf of rock dams a pool of thick greenish liquid. A humanoid body in torn robes with one arm chewed off is ominously propped against the ledge.

This area conceals the entrance to the Devourer cult's hidden base, the Star-Eater's Spine. Squares with ash in them are difficult terrain. The rocky shelf to the northwest is about 3 feet tall and provides cover as a low obstacle. The 5-foot-deep pool behind the shelf is a mixture of ash, water, and toxic chemicals, and it's highly acidic. Anyone who touches the pool takes 2d6 acid damage each round she is in contact with it. Anyone who swims in the pool (or becomes otherwise fully submerged in it) takes 10d6 acid damage per round.

A PC who succeeds at a DC 20 Perception check finds a trapdoor in the ground hidden beneath the piles of silvery ash in the middle of the chamber. The trapdoor opens into an underground tunnel that leads to the Star-Eater's Spine (area **B**).

Creature: A skreesire lairs here, lurking in the acid pool. The cult used the creature as a guardian to protect the entrance to their base (see area **A4**), and it now dominates this expanse of the asteroid. Once it detects intruders, the skreesire becomes obsessed with destroying them. As soon as the PCs enter this area, the skreesire targets a random PC with its enthrall ability, suggesting that the character venture closer to the acid pool to see what treasures might lie within. If the PC fails her saving throw and approaches the pool, the skreesire tries to grab her with its tentacles and reposition her into the acid. If the PC succeeds at her saving throw and the party hasn't already attacked it, the skreesire tries to target a second PC in this way.

If any of the skreelings from area **A2** survive, one or more of them might join the fight if they are in a position to be able to hear it.

SKREESIRE CR 7

XP 3,200

HP 100 (see page 57)

TACTICS

During Combat The skreesire pulls itself onto the rocky ledge and attacks with its tentacles. When it successfully grapples a creature, it attempts a reposition combat maneuver to try to drop that creature into the acid pool.

Morale The skreesire is supremely confident in its combat skills and is already incensed that it has lost its regular supply of cultist sacrifices. It fights to the death.

Treasure: The body propped against the ledge beside the acid pool is wearing an unholy symbol around its neck depicting a black hole with a red center (identifiable as the symbol of the Devourer with a successful DC 15 Mysticism check). A PC who succeeds at a DC 15 Medicine check can determine that the corpse is very fresh; likely only a few days old. The corpse was one of the last Devourer cultists to flee the secret base. With so many cultists pouring out of the base and leaving in starships, the skreesire realized that the cult was abandoning its underground lair. Angered that the cult broke its agreement with no opportunity for recompense or recourse, the skreesire began attacking cultists as they emerged from the trapdoor. This unlucky cultist was not fast enough to avoid the skreesire's wrath. The cultist is carrying a satchel containing a hefty collection of various rare coins worth 1,200 credits.

A4. Cultists' Demise

This expansive alcove is devoid of the silvery ash that's prevalent elsewhere on the asteroid, but it has the appearance of a gruesome graveyard. Several discarded corpses lie here—some that look just a few days old, and some that are rotting with the telltale signs of weeks, if not months, of decay.

This horrible scene is evidence of the dark pact that the Devourer cult made with the skreesire in area **A3**. Although brutal, the mind-controlling beast is canny, and the cultists were able to offer it an enticing deal when they set up their underground base on this asteroid: the skreesire agreed to let the cultists enter and exit their base as they pleased, and the cultists promised to sacrifice one of their own to the creature every few months. The skreesire implanted its fleshy egg sacs in the corpses of these sacrifices, which then hatched into skreelings (the current clutch of which currently inhabits area **A2**).

If the PCs examine the corpses and succeed at a DC 15 Medicine check, they discover that the cultists were killed in a methodical, ritualistic manner before being flayed and implanted with something after death. If the PCs have already identified the skreesire in area **A3**, they can determine that it inflicted the postmortem wounds.

Treasure: Sifting through the corpses is gruesome work, but there are still a few items of value on the bodies. A PC who succeeds at a DC 15 Perception check finds an onyx-and-ruby ankle bracelet worth 1,150 credits on one of the bodies. A PC who succeeds at a DC 20 Perception check discovers a small pocket of valuables sewn into a robe worn by one of the corpses, containing a *glove of storing* and a collection of several credsticks holding a total of 800 credits.

SYMBOL OF THE DEVOURER

A5. Shard-Filled Slope

Nestled between a sheer cliff and a small, narrow rock formation, the ground here slopes at odd angles. To the north is a small field pocked with shards of metal, their sharp edges gleaming. To the west, a steep incline leads upward to a cave-like structure.

Both slopes here (east and downward to the landing area, west and upward to area **A4**) are considered difficult terrain. The chunks of metal are left over from the failed mining operation on this asteroid decades ago. The shards' edges are quite sharp and deal 1d4 slashing damage to anyone who touches one.

Treasure: A PC who inspects the metallic shards and succeeds at a DC 15 Physical Science check can identify the composition of the metal as cold iron (*Core Rulebook* 191). If the shards are extracted from the ground, they can be used as cold iron improvised weapons (*Core Rulebook* 169) that deal slashing damage—useful for overcoming the damage reduction of the skreelings in area **A2** and the skreesire in area **A3**. Beyond their potential use as weapons, the cold iron shards can be gathered and sold for the valuable ore they contain. In total, 10 bulk worth of cold iron ore can be collected, worth 1,125 credits.

In addition, a PC who succeeds at a DC 18 Perception check notices a silvery glint on the ground among the metallic shards, which turns out to be a dented silver amulet with an oval pendant and a red stone embedded in its center. This pendant is worth only about 25 credits, but a successful DC 15 Mysticism check reveals that it's an unholy symbol of the Devourer—hinting at the presence of cultists who have since fled the asteroid.

Once the PCs discover the hidden trapdoor in area **A3**, they can explore the subterranean Devourer cult base called the Star-Eater's Spine. While the PCs might expect to encounter hordes of cultists here, they soon find that the base is eerily abandoned. Why and where the cult has fled are questions the PCs must seek answers for, as well as whether other dark parties are interested, and why.

B. THE STAR-EATER'S SPINE

This underground bunker once was home to a powerful Devourer cult that had its fingers in many sinister schemes, including obsessively seeking information about an unholy prophecy the cultists hold sacred. Now it is almost entirely deserted. As soon as the cultists connected the Gate of Twelve Suns and Stellar Degenerator with Nejeor, they fled the Diaspora for that distant system—but not without leaving a few security measures in place.

The entire base is constructed inside an old underground mining tunnel; the cultists lined the unworked stone walls of the tunnel with reinforced concrete supported with steel beams. The ceilings are 15 feet high and the doors are unlocked, unless otherwise noted. In contrast to the thin atmosphere of the asteroid, inside the base the atmosphere is of normal pressure and composition to support most oxygen-breathing life-forms so the cultists could occupy the base without space suits or other environmental protections; however, the area remains one of low gravity.

The backup generator that powers the base's life support and defensive systems is still running, but since the cult doesn't plan to return anytime soon, the entirety of the base's interior dark unless otherwise indicated (although the lights can be switched back on using the terminal in area **B2**).

The PCs are not the first noncultists to recently explore this base, however. That honor belongs to members of the Corpse Fleet, who managed to deftly avoid the skreesire and skreelings in area **A**. There are a few hints that the Corpse Fleet made it to the base first (namely in areas **B3** and **B10**), but it should become clear to the PCs that they're not alone in their interest in the cult's base when they examine the computer in area **B11**, and later when they're accosted by Corpse Fleet ships upon leaving the Star-Eater's Spine (see **Event 2**).

B1. Foyer of the Void (CR 7)

The dark and oppressive tunnel below the asteroid's surface gives way to a severe chamber crafted of metal and concrete. A wide sliding door stands in the far wall of the room, rust dappling its edges like rotten lace. A single light above the doorway flickers weakly.

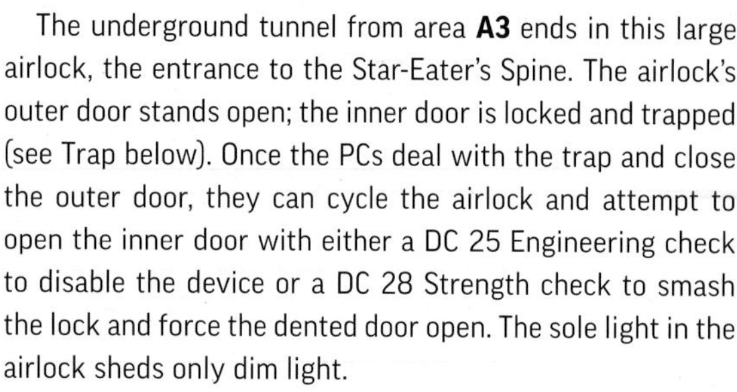

The underground tunnel from area **A3** ends in this large airlock, the entrance to the Star-Eater's Spine. The airlock's outer door stands open; the inner door is locked and trapped (see Trap below). Once the PCs deal with the trap and close the outer door, they can cycle the airlock and attempt to open the inner door with either a DC 25 Engineering check to disable the device or a DC 28 Strength check to smash the lock and force the dented door open. The sole light in the airlock sheds only dim light.

Trap: Before abandoning the Star-Eater's Spine, the Devourer cultists hastily locked the inner airlock door and rigged a trap to discourage unwanted visitors to their base. As entropy of the mind is the cultists' specialty, they brewed a concoction that drives intelligent creatures mad, then rigged a contraption to spray the mixture through a vent above the door when sensors detect the body heat of living creatures within 10 feet of the door. Any environmental protections from a creature's armor do nothing to avoid this trap's effects, since it's specifically designed to penetrate breathing apparatuses (the undead agents of the Corpse Fleet were immune to the spores and thus ignored the trap).

MIND SPORES TRAP — CR 7

XP 3,200

Type hybrid; **Perception** DC 30; **Disable** Computers DC 27 (from computer in area **B2** only), Engineering DC 25 (jam vent closed), or Mysticism DC 25 (neutralize spores)

Trigger proximity (thermal, 10 feet); **Reset** 1 hour or manual (computer in area **B2**)

Effect mind spores (–4 penalty to Intelligence-, Wisdom-, and Charisma-based ability checks, skill checks, and saving throws for 1d4 hours; this is a mind-affecting effect); Will DC 17 negates; multiple targets (all targets in 30-ft. cone)

B2. Operations Terminal

Riveted walls of steel around the airlock hatch extend into a cavernous gloom. At the chamber's center stands a wide computer console that practically stretches to the ceiling. Rows of grimy buttons frame its blank display screen, from which emanates the faintest of glows.

This computer terminal controls the electrical mainframe, life-support systems, and major defense mechanisms of the Star-Eater's Spine. It is a tier 3 computer, requiring a successful DC 25 Computers check to hack (if the PCs have the security key card found in area **B6c**, they gain a +5 bonus to the check). Once the PCs have access to the computer, they can easily restore light to the base. However, the base's lighting system is in a state of disrepair, and turning the lights back on increases the illumination level throughout the complex only to dim light.

In addition, the computer has control modules for two curious systems: one is labeled "Entrance Deterrent" and the other "Chamber of Devouring." The former controls the mind spores trap in area **B1**, while the latter controls the laser wall trap in area **B3**. Both control modules are behind firewall countermeasures. Accessing either of the modules requires a successful DC 27 Computers check (the security key card from area **B6c** provides a +5 bonus to these checks), and PCs who gain access to the modules can reset or permanently disable the associated traps.

Beyond these functions, it is clear that this terminal merely controls the base's operating systems and does not contain any of the cult's logs or sensitive operating data. There are oblique references in the code to a larger and more comprehensive computer network located somewhere deeper in the base that contains this information as well as the cult's comm logs. If the PCs don't realize it on their own, a successful DC 10 Intelligence check reveals that any information about where the cultists went and what exactly they might have learned on Castrovel would be located in that larger computer system.

Story Award: Award the PCs XP as normal for disabling either of the traps through the computer's control modules, though they can receive XP for each trap only once; if the PCs have already triggered or disabled either of the traps, they do not get additional XP for activating or disabling them again.

B3. Chamber of Devouring (CR 7)

Half a dozen tiered pillars are interspersed throughout this wide hallway, which ends in a concave wall made of plated steel. A strange pile of body parts and viscera lies next to the easternmost pillar. The faint scent of ozone hangs in the air.

The cultists practiced profane rituals in the Devourer's name in this unholy chamber and punished any who stood against them. They were especially fond of forcing enemies into this room's western end before triggering the most deadly feature of the entire base: the laser wall trap that runs the length of the room (see Trap below).

The tiered pillars are 10 feet tall and constructed of treated adamantine alloy. If the PCs investigate the mass of gore next to the eastern pillar, with a successful DC 15 Mysticism check they can identify it as the remains of some manner of undead humanoid. It's difficult to discern the creature's exact features, however, because the corpse has been cut into little chunks (a result of the room's laser wall trap).

Trap: The trap in this room consists of a latticed wall of laser beams, stretching from floor to ceiling and wall to wall, that triggers when a creature moves past the easternmost pillar. One round later on the trap's initiative count, the laser wall activates, beginning at the eastern end of the room (marked by a white dashed line on the map) and rapidly

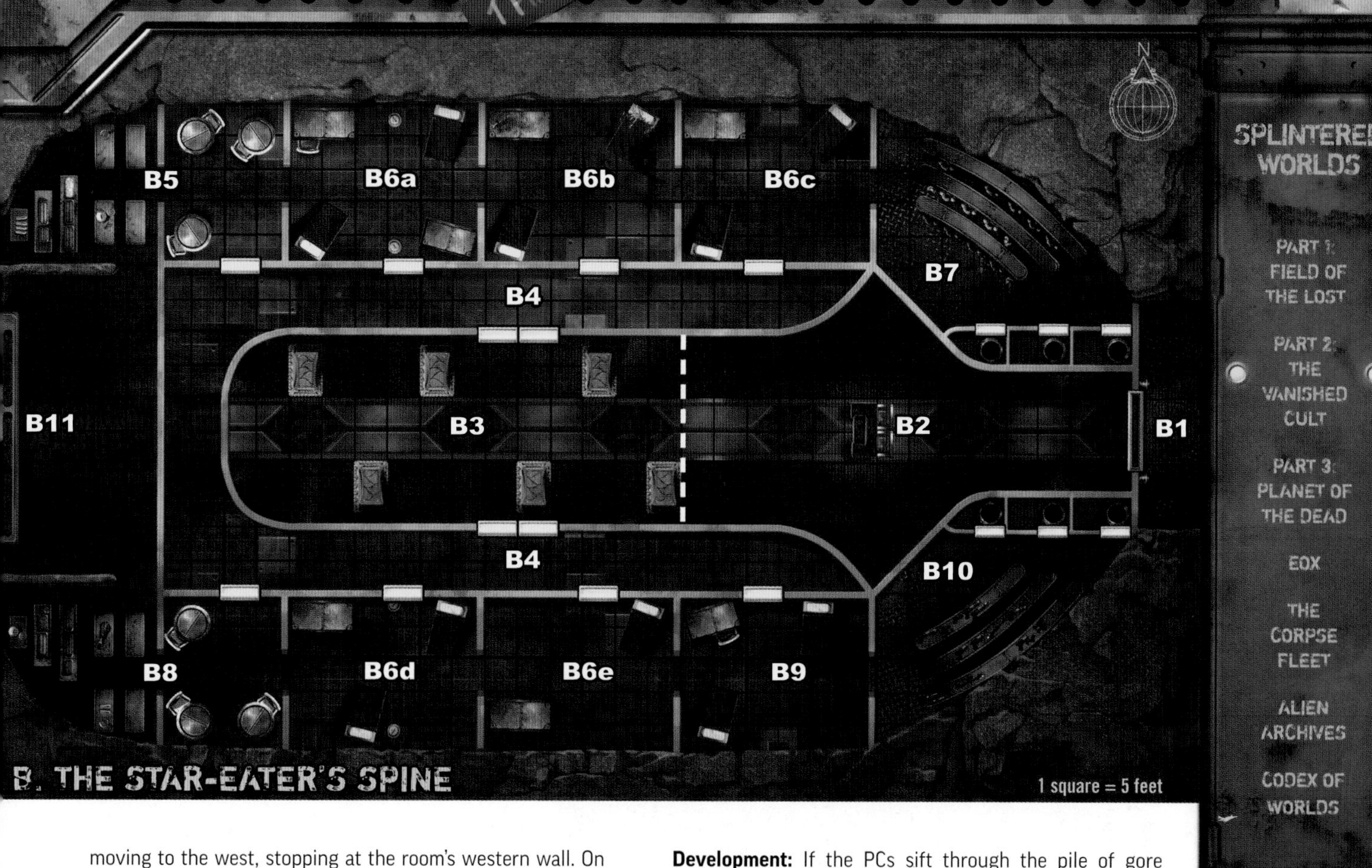

moving to the west, stopping at the room's western wall. On the following round, the laser wall moves back to the east, stopping where it began, just beyond the easternmost pillar. This process continues each round until the trap is disabled from the computer terminal in area **B2**.

The room's pillars are treated with a coating that deflects the trap's laser beams. Moving through the room while the trap is active is possible, but it requires a successful Reflex saving throw on the trap's initiative count to avoid the lasers by darting behind one of the pillars when the laser wall passes. A creature must attempt this saving throw each round it remains in the Chamber of Devouring.

There is a high price to pay for sluggishness in avoiding the laser wall. If a creature rolls a natural 1 on the Reflex saving throw to avoid the trap, it must attempt a DC 15 Reflex saving throw. If the creature succeeds at this second saving throw, it takes normal damage from the trap. If it fails this second saving throw, the creature takes 20d6 fire damage as the laser wall slices through it, and is likely sliced into minuscule chunks of gore.

MOVING LASER WALL — CR 7

XP 3,200

Type technological; **Perception** DC 30; **Disable** Computers DC 27 (from computer in area **B2** only)

Trigger location; **Initiative** +12; **Duration** continuous (until disabled); **Reset** manual (computer in area **B2**)

Initial Effect wall of laser beams (5d10 F); Reflex DC 17 avoids (see above if natural 1 is rolled); onset delay (1 round); multiple targets (all targets in area **B3**)

Development: If the PCs sift through the pile of gore near the pillar, they can find a mostly intact patch from the creature's environment suit. A PC who succeeds at a DC 20 Culture check recognizes that the patch identifies the creature as a member of the Corpse Fleet, the exiled remnant of the Eoxian Navy (see the Corpse Fleet sidebar on page 14 for more information the PCs might know about the Corpse Fleet). This is a clue that the Corpse Fleet preceded the PCs in infiltrating the Star-Eater's Spine.

B4. Access Corridors

A cloying gloom fills this long, claustrophobic hallway. A red light on the western wall blinks slowly, giving the scene a sinister atmosphere.

These corridors afford access to the base's mess halls and kitchens (areas **B5** and **B8**) and living quarters for the cultists (areas **B6** and **B9**).

B5. North Mess

This area is divided into two wings. The western chamber contains several pantry shelves as well as four flat, utilitarian stove units with attached faucets, while the eastern side is filled with round metal tables and chairs.

This is one of two main kitchen and dining areas to serve the cultists inhabiting the Star-Eater's Spine, along with the south mess (area **B8**). The pantry shelves mostly hold dry and

THE CORPSE FLEET

The first time the PCs come across evidence of the Corpse Fleet's involvement in the situation, allow them to attempt Culture checks to recall knowledge. The PCs learn all of the following with a DC less than or equal to the result of the check. PCs whose home world is Eox or who have spent significant time on the undead planet gain a +10 circumstance bonus to this check.

Culture Check Result	Knowledge Recalled
20+	The Corpse Fleet is an exiled offshoot of the Eoxian Navy that's made up of powerful admirals and captains who roam the universe in starships forged from bone and steel. Officially, the government of Eox condemns this rogue organization.
24+	The Corpse Fleet formed when powerful and disgruntled members of the Eoxian Navy could not stomach their world's adoption of the Absalom Pact. These naval officers deeply believed in the same sort of Eoxian superiority that once led the planet to destroy civilizations that refused to acknowledge Eox's power—including the worlds known as the Twins, the shattered remnants of which now form the Diaspora.
28+	Although Eox's government and ambassadors to the Pact Worlds make a grandiose show of denouncing the Corpse Fleet, rumors claim that some of the powerful Eoxian rulers known as bone sages still clandestinely communicate with the exiles, and perhaps even secretly aid them with their work to promote Eoxian supremacy. The general population on Eox seems largely ambivalent—perhaps suspiciously so—toward the exiled fleet.

CORPSE FLEET INSIGNIA

preserved foods, as the cultists didn't devote much time to packing their supplies before heading to Nejeor. The nature of the supplies here is odd, with extremely spicy options mixed with bizarre strains of fruit and vegetable preserves. However, there are enough palatable options that PCs can spend 1d4 hours preparing the foods here into a good meal that can feed up to eight individuals. Alternatively, the PCs can instead spend 30 minutes arranging the stores into up to eight R2E meal packets that can be consumed at their leisure.

B6. Living Quarters

Minimalist sleeping pallets lie on the severe metal floor of this room, and simple shelves and dressers serve as furniture.

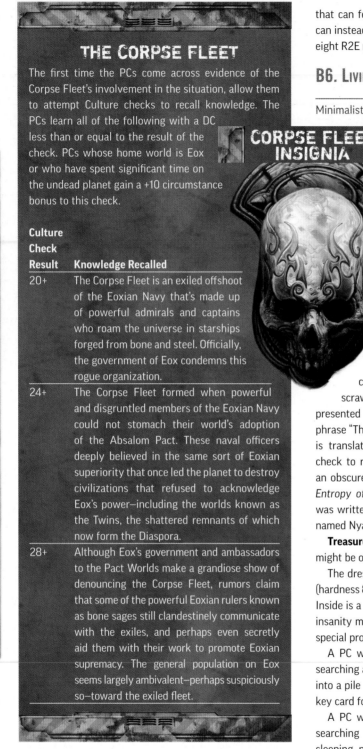

These chambers were the personal living quarters and prayer rooms of the cultists of the Star-Eater's Spine. They are mostly identical, though strange iconography is scattered throughout them, from profane altars made of skulls to metal sculptures depicting swirling shapes tinged with some dark, foul substance. Strange garbled phrases are written in a variety of colored paints on several walls.

The graffiti on the walls is written in Abyssal; if no one can speak that language, the PCs can translate it with a successful DC 20 Culture check to decipher writing. Although the graffiti is scrawled in different handwriting and is sometimes presented out of order, the writing essentially repeats the phrase "The Entropy of Existence is known." Once this phrase is translated, a PC who succeeds at a DC 25 Mysticism check to recall knowledge realizes it's likely a reference to an obscure holy text of the Cult of the Devourer called *The Entropy of Existence and Glorious Rise of the Void*, which was written some centuries ago by an evil elven soothsayer named Nyara and contains ominous prophecies.

Treasure: Three of the living quarters contain items that might be of interest to the PCs.

The dresser in the northwest corner of area **B6b** is locked (hardness 8, HP 15, break DC 16, Engineering DC 18 to disable). Inside is a pair of injection gloves and 2 doses of weaponized insanity mist that can be used in weapons with the injection special property.

A PC who succeeds at a DC 16 Perception check while searching area **B6c** discovers a thin white plastic card tucked into a pile of discarded clothes on the floor. This is a security key card for the computer in area **B2**.

A PC who succeeds at a DC 16 Perception check while searching area **B6d** finds a small lump under one of the sleeping pallets, which turns out to be a datapad and a credstick holding 1,400 credits. The datapad is a tier 1 computer, requiring a successful DC 17 Computers check to hack the system to gain access. Among the mundane data files, electronic messages, gaming applications, and other files on the datapad is a single video file labeled "Do Not Delete," which the PCs can notice with a successful DC 10 Perception check once they have access. In the video, a verthani and a gnome are sitting cross-legged on the floor inside one of the base's living quarters. Both are dressed in robes and wearing unholy symbols of the Devourer, and the verthani is teaching the gnome to sing a paean to the Devourer. Throughout the song, both cultists repeat the phrase "Nyara knows!" over and over. A PC who succeeds at a DC 25 Mysticism check to recall knowledge recognizes Nyara as the name of an ancient elven soothsayer who was most notoriously the author of a Devourer cult holy text called *The Entropy of Existence and Glorious Rise of the Void*. This is far more than just a simple instructional video, however, though the PCs likely will not recognize its significance at this point. In fact, the repeated phrase "Nyara knows!" is a password for accessing the base's datacore (see area **B11** for more details).

B7. Armory (CR 6)

Three largely empty rows of shelves line the northeastern side of this wide room. Here and there, a drooping suit of armor hangs from its rack, suggesting that this room once provided storage of a more martial bent.

This room once stored the cult's collection of body armor, though its members took most of the pieces with them when they fled the base. Three doors to the south each provide access to a cramped water closet.

Creatures: The cultists left two patrol-class security robots here to deter any who might disturb their headquarters. The robots activate as soon as any creature enters the room. They follow intruders throughout the base and fight until destroyed.

PATROL-CLASS SECURITY ROBOTS (2) CR 4
XP 1,200 each
HP 52 each (*Starfinder Alien Archive* 94)

Treasure: The shelves hold two d-suits I, two estex suits II, two suits of kasatha microcord II, and a ysoki refractor suit. All these suits of armor are broken (*Core Rulebook* 273) and decorated distastefully with skulls, fangs, and other strange Devourer symbols, but they can be repaired and the dark decorations can be removed without no unexpected difficulty.

A PC who succeeds at a DC 20 Perception check detects a hidden panel in the northeast wall. The panel is locked (hardness 20, HP 60, break DC 28, Engineering DC 20 to disable), but opening it reveals a suit of golemforged plating III with jump jets installed.

B8. South Mess

This kitchen and dining area seem as if they were abandoned in the middle of a meal's preparation. Pots of meat slurry and festering dairy sit on the stoves to the west, and metal cups full of some sludgy, long-turned beverage sit on the tables to the east. Tiny flies buzz about the entire scene, flitting from place to place among the rotten smorgasbord.

The cultists had been in the beginning stages of assembling dinner when they received Tahomen's communication from Castrovel. Sensing that a key prophecy of their profane religion was at hand, they hastily threw some prepared foods in heat-containment units, left other partially prepared meals to rot, and fled with whatever else they could grab on their way out of the base. The north mess (area **B5**) was not yet in use for the evening when the cultists fled, hence the

SECURITY ROBOT

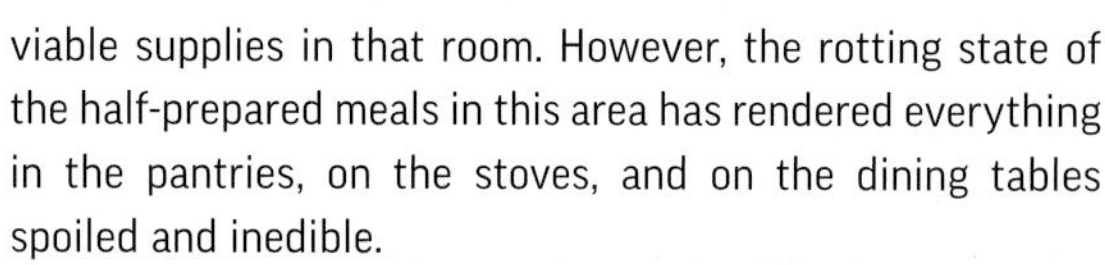

viable supplies in that room. However, the rotting state of the half-prepared meals in this area has rendered everything in the pantries, on the stoves, and on the dining tables spoiled and inedible.

Hazard: When the PCs enter this area, they must succeed at DC 18 Fortitude saving throws or be sickened by the horrible stench of rotting food for 10 minutes. PCs affected by the rotten smorgasbord cannot rest to regain Stamina Points during this 10-minute period.

B9. Trapped Quarters (CR 5)

This room resembles the base's other living quarters (area **B6**).

Trap: The cultists who lived here were engineers who helped design the elaborate laser wall trap in area **B3**, and they outfitted the dresser in the room's northwest corner with a smaller laser trap, which blasts an arc of laser beams when any of the dresser's drawers are opened.

LASER ARC TRAP — CR 5

XP 1,600

Type technological; **Perception** DC 27; **Disable** Engineering DC 22

Trigger touch; **Reset** manual

Effect laser arc (4d10+5 F); Reflex DC 15 half

Treasure: The cultists found it difficult to bypass their own trap, so they were forced to leave their belongings behind when the cult abandoned the base. The dresser contains the cultists' collection of armor upgrades and weapon fusion seals: a brown force field, a mk I electrostatic field, a *bleeding fusion seal* (6th), and a *vicious fusion seal* (5th; *Starfinder Adventure Path* #2 53).

B10. Arsenal

Three rows of mostly bare shelves stand along the southeastern end of this wide room. Here and there, a dilapidated pistol or longarm sits on a dusty shelf. Three humanoid robots stand near the north wall; each is hunched over and covered in scorch marks, occasionally emitting puffs of sickly gray smoke.

This room once stored the cult's collection of stolen and looted weapons, though its members took most of the firepower with them when they fled the base. Three doors to the north each lead into a small water closet.

The three robots are clearly disabled; if the PCs examine them and succeed at a DC 16 Engineering check, they can identify the constructs as security robots and determine that gunfire—likely lasers—violently dispatched them sometime within the past week. If the PCs encountered the active security robots in area **B7**, they recognize these bots as the same model, likely programmed to protect the arsenal even in the cultists' absence.

Further, a PC who succeeds at a DC 18 Perception check while examining the scene finds a small, strange technological device covered in leathery gore. With a successful DC 24 Engineering or Mysticism check, the PCs can identify the device as a necrograft—an augmentation using undead organs and necromantic rituals rather than cybernetics or biotech—that was installed in an undead creature (see page 42 for more information). A PC who succeeds at a DC 20 Culture check knows that necrotech is commonly available on Eox and quite popular among members of the Corpse Fleet—though nothing definitively links the augmentation found here to the exiled navy.

Treasure: The shelves here hold the following battered weapons: a pulsecaster pistol, a red star plasma rifle, a tactical acid dart rifle, a thunderstrike sonic pistol, and a utility scattergun. All of the weapons are unloaded and broken (*Core Rulebook* 273), but they can be repaired.

B11. Datacore (CR 6)

Looming over the west side of this sterile room are floor-to-ceiling computer consoles that swallow the entire wall with dizzying displays of darkened screens, inset buttons, levers, and switches. A squat, bony, reptilian creature is slumped over in a congealed puddle of blood in front of the consoles.

This room houses the Star-Eater's Spine's datacore, the primary computer network used by the Devourer cultists here, as well as a surviving guardian left behind by the cult (see Creature on page 18). A PC can identify the dead creature in the middle of the room as a veolisk with a successful DC 19 Mysticism check.

The datacore is a tier 3 computer with several secure data modules and a control module for the base's system-wide comm unit. Accessing the datacore requires a successful DC 25 Computers check to hack the system. Anyone attempting to hack the computer realizes the system normally requires a voiceprint password, meaning an authorized user must speak a password to gain access. If the PCs found the "Do Not Delete" video file on the datapad in area **B6d**, they can play the video to enter the computer's password ("Nyara knows!") with one of the cultist's voiceprints, granting them a +5 bonus to Computers checks to hack the system (including accessing the secure data modules described below).

Once the PCs have accessed the system, three data modules likely interest them, labeled respectively "Activities," "Intelligence," and "Sacred Lore." The contents of these data modules are described in the following entries, though some of them are protected by security countermeasures. If a module has such countermeasures, they are detailed at the beginning of the module's entry.

Activities Data Module: This module can be accessed without additional Computers checks. It states the mission of this sect of the Cult of the Devourer in no uncertain terms.

The denizens of the Star-Eater's Spine were devoted to poring through the prophecies in a sacred but cryptic tome called *The Entropy of Existence and Glorious Rise of the Void*. The data contains the cult's analysis of some of these divinations, including one prophecy flagged as high-priority. This high-priority prophecy is not stored in this data module, but a link points to its location in another secure data module labeled "Sacred Lore" (see below). The cultists focused on this one prophecy in particular because they thought it the most likely candidate for them to bring to fruition. From the data, it appears the cultists interpreted the prophecy as referring to some sort of weapon—one powerful enough to serve as a "key" to untold destruction—but they have deciphered little else. In addition to the cultists' obsessive work to understand more of this prophecy's latent instructions, this module details the terrible, ritualistic tortures (such as the laser wall in area **B3**) the cult enacted to try to pull further clues from those lines.

Intelligence Data Module: Because of the sensitive information it contains, this secure data module is protected behind a firewall and equipped with a feedback countermeasure. Hacking the Intelligence module requires a successful DC 27 Computers check. If a PC fails this check by 5 or more, every device used in the hacking attempt is infected with a virus that imparts a –5 penalty to all skill checks using the infected equipment. Disabling the feedback countermeasure or removing the virus from an affected device requires a successful DC 25 Computers check.

The Intelligence data module contains records of all of the communications between the Star-Eater's Spine and the Devourer cult on Castrovel (see *Starfinder Adventure Path #2: Temple of the Twelve*). Although it appears that the cultists tried to erase this data before they deserted the base, by successfully hacking this module, the PCs also recover most of the communication logs for the base's comm unit. These captioned recordings document the Castrovelian cult leader Tahomen's boastful crowing about his cult's activities at the Temple of the Twelve, including a premature (and ultimately untrue) claim of the cult's humiliating defeat of the PCs. The last communication log, however, takes on a triumphantly gleeful tone. In it, Tahomen reports that information in the temple's inner sanctum has revealed the location of the "key" emphasized in Nyara's prophecy. In the final line of the recording, Tahomen jubilantly states, "Our future awaits, far beyond the confines of the Star-Eater's Spine! You must fly, my sisters and brothers! Fly to (garbled static), where the Key awaits..." The recording then ends.

Successfully hacking the data module reveals that the name of the location the cultists fled to was deliberately deleted and then meticulously scrubbed from the system. The electronic signature of the hacker who performed these tasks is unlike any of the digital footprints left in either this datacore or the computer terminal in area **B2**. However, there are clear signs that this data was deleted just a few days ago—sometime after the cultists abandoned the Star-Eater's Spine, given physical clues left behind at the base, such as the state of the mess hall in area **B8**.

Sacred Lore Data Module: This module is secured behind a firewall, requiring a DC 27 Computers check to successfully hack. It contains reams of information about the cult's profane belief in the Devourer, the assured entropy of the universe, and the cultists' unholy roles in bringing about the end of existence for the glory of their dark religion. In addition to general religious dogma and near-mad ramblings, the data module also details the

Star-Eater's Spine cult's fascination with an ancient elven soothsayer named Nyara, outlining her history as detailed in the first two paragraphs of the Adventure Background on page 3. The data even includes a computer-generated hologram of Nyara recounting some of her most enigmatic prognostications, as recorded in her most infamous book, *The Entropy of Existence and Glorious Rise of the Void*, which the cultists of the Star-Eater's Spine treat as gospel. One of these predictions is flagged as high-priority; if that prediction is accessed, the hologram of Nyara recites, "In the maw of the Twelve lies the Key. Forsooth, shall all be undone. When the knee meets the gorge, so far. The widening gyre implodes—magnificently." An annotation on the file points to the cult's study of this prophecy stored in the datacore's Activities data module (see page 16).

Creature: The Devourer cultists kept two reptilian beasts called veolisks in this room. Considered sacred creatures by the cult, the monsters both defended the base and played key roles in some profane rituals, but due to the veolisks' dangerous unpredictability, the cultists opted not to bring their pets with them when they fled the base. When Corpse Fleet agents recently explored the Star-Eater's Spine, they dispatched one of the veolisks, leaving its partner here to stew in its small-minded rage, seeking any outlet possible for its destructive void gaze. The PCs provide the creature with the perfect opportunity to cause suffering and mayhem, and it attacks them on sight.

VEOLISK **CR 6**

XP 2,400

HP 90 (see page 60)

Development: It was, in fact, the Corpse Fleet that erased the data in the Intelligence data module that reveals the Cult of the Devourer abandoned the Star-Eater's Spine to travel to the Nejeor system in search of the Gate of Twelve Suns. Due to that redaction, at this point, the PCs have no way of knowing where the cultists fled or who exactly deleted the name of their destination, though they may have strong suspicions about the latter, in which case the PCs likely have good reason to believe that the trail to the Gate of Twelve Suns and the Stellar Degenerator leads to Eox. In any event, they'll have more than enough reason to head there after their upcoming encounter with the Corpse Fleet (see **Event 2**).

Story Award: If the PCs successfully hack the Intelligence data module and learn that someone else accessed the Star-Eater's Spine's computer system after the cult deserted the base, award them 1,600 XP.

EVENT 2: CORPSE FLEET AMBUSH (CR 4)

The PCs can leave the Star-Eater's Spine at any time to return to their ship, and the journey back through area **A** is uneventful unless they left any threats behind on their way in. The PCs might decide to contact Chiskisk with their findings about the Devourer cultists and the signposts pointing to Eox that they turned up at the Star-Eater's Spine. You should encourage PCs to come up with their own plans for tracking the cultists. Before they can leave the Diaspora, however, the PCs discover that elements of the Corpse Fleet still linger nearby.

Starship Combat: The Corpse Fleet has left behind two tiny ships with orders to keep any meddlers from following their agents out of the Diaspora. The two interceptors are not capable of Drift travel, but the pilots have been promised that a larger carrier ship will be sent in a few weeks' time to retrieve them and return them to the fleet. As a result, the elebrian bone trooper pilots are fiercely determined to annihilate any interlopers who might have designs on following the Corpse Fleet and prove themselves to their superiors.

From hidden positions behind neighboring asteroids, the Eoxians saw the PCs land on Asteroid K9204 and then descend down into the Star-Eater's Spine. The undead have spent the ensuing time planning how to best ambush the PCs and their ship, since they figure that's the best way to rid the Corpse Fleet of its troublesome tail. As soon as the PCs power up their ship and leave the asteroid's surface, the two interceptors reveal their presence and open fire on the PCs' ship.

This encounter uses the starship combat rules beginning on page 316 of the *Starfinder Core Rulebook*. The two Corpse Fleet ships are Death's Head Necrogliders. A PC can identify the make and model of the two interceptors with a successful DC 11 Engineering check to identify technology. In addition, a PC who succeeds at a DC 15 Culture check recognizes the ships as Corpse Fleet vessels.

DEATH'S HEAD NECROGLIDERS (2) **TIER 1/2**

Starfinder Core Rulebook 306

HP 30 each

Development: If the PCs defeat both Corpse Fleet ships, they can capture and interrogate the pilots. The two bone trooper pilots deny their membership in the Corpse Fleet, though their uniforms and the markings on their ships belie their claim. If coerced, the pilots can confirm that the Corpse Fleet did visit the Star-Eater's Spine and that they were ordered to attack anyone leaving the base—information that certainly implicates the Corpse Fleet as the party behind the deleted data in the base's datacore (see area **B11**). Unfortunately, neither pilot has any knowledge of the Corpse Fleet's goals in investigating the cult base, and they don't know the ultimate destination of either the Corpse Fleet or the Cult of the Devourer. If necessary, statistics for the bone troopers can be found on page 56 of *Starfinder Adventure Path* #1. If the PCs haven't already recalled the information they might know about the Corpse Fleet, allow them to attempt Culture checks to recall knowledge as described in the Corpse Fleet sidebar on page 14.

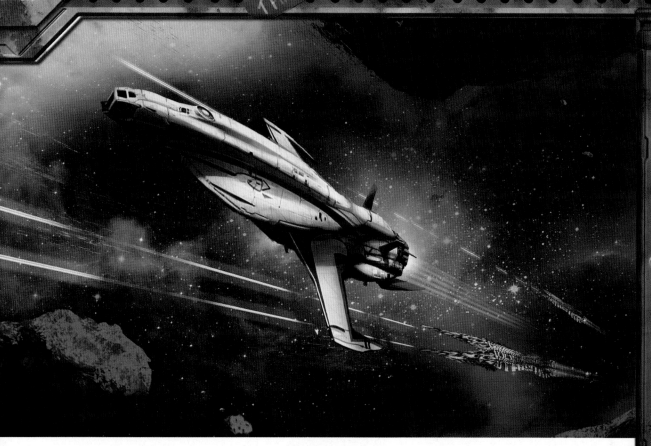

Story Award: If the PCs defeat or escape the Corpse Fleet Necrogliders, award them 1,200 XP.

With the Cult of the Devourer having departed to parts unknown, the Corpse Fleet is likely the PCs' only remaining lead, as tenuous as it may be. Fortunately, the PCs should already be planning to go to Eox, where they can follow up on their Corpse Fleet leads. If the PCs do not immediately decide to go to Eox to try to learn what the Corpse Fleet knows (and where its agents, and the Cult of the Devourer, have gone), Chiskisk contacts them and strongly suggests that they do so (see below).

TRANSMISSION FROM CHISKISK

Shortly after the PCs' encounter with the Corpse Fleet ships in **Event 2** and before they reach Eox, they receive a transmission from Chiskisk, their Starfinder Society contact on Absalom Station. Due to the time lags involved in interplanetary communication (*Core Rulebook* 430), the message was prerecorded, so the PCs will not be able to respond in real time. The following exchange assumes the PCs have already informed Chiskisk of their run-ins with the Corpse Fleet. If this is not the case, you'll need to adjust the following text. Read or paraphrase the following when the PCs play Chiskisk's message.

"Greetings, my friends. It is a grave matter, indeed, that the Corpse Fleet seems so intent on keeping you from following the Cult of the Devourer's trail, even to the point of attempting to eliminate you," Chiskisk begins, their antennae folded pensively. "I presume that means they are now searching for the Stellar Degenerator as well. The Corpse Fleet is not to be trifled with, and its schemes perpetually frustrate the Eoxians here on Absalom Station. The Eoxian delegation diligently reports the efforts their planet undertakes to curb the Corpse Fleet's activities, but they never seem to make a dent in the threat.

"Given your run-ins with the Corpse Fleet of late, I have kept my antennae in the air. My contacts in the Eoxian embassy here on the station have worked with a bureaucrat and historian in Eox's Ministry of Eternal Vigilance named Waneda Trux. She is posted in the city of Orphys and handles reports about Corpse Fleet activity on Eox. According to my contacts, Ms. Trux recently received some indications that the fleet's agents are up to something—perhaps recruiting for a big mission or gathering resources. It's unclear. But following any leads that Ms. Trux has gathered could very well reveal the Corpse Fleet's plots for the Stellar Degenerator and, if we are lucky, the coordinates where the cultists from the Star-Eater's Spine fled to.

"Waneda Trux's office is located in a district of Orphys

called the Splice. I have informed her that you will be arriving soon. I will not misrepresent Eox—it is a dead world, and it will not be comfortable, even for representatives of the Starfinder Society on official business. But Eox is a member of the Pact Worlds, so one can expect a certain amount of civilization."

Chiskisk clears their throat with a metallic rasp and continues. "I am sure I do not need to remind you, but this mission is of the utmost priority. You must meet Waneda Trux and find the location of this Stellar Degenerator. You must keep it out of the hands of the Corpse Fleet and the Cult of the Devourer. Everything could be at stake.

"End transmission."

The PCs will likely have questions for Chiskisk at this point, though the transmission time of 1d6–1 hours for each message makes it more like exchanging letters than holding a conversation. Fortunately, the journey to Eox takes a minimum of 1d6 days, so there should be enough time for the PCs to get all the answers they need before they reach their destination. Below are Chiskisk's answers to some of the PCs' likely questions. If the PCs ask Chiskisk for more information about the Corpse Fleet, the shirren can relay any of the information from the Corpse Fleet sidebar on page 14 that the PCs did not recall on their own.

Who is Waneda Trux? "Waneda is a ghoul," Chiskisk says, "but she was once human and a resident of Absalom Station. Her relatively recent transition to undeath makes her slightly more accommodating to the Starfinder Society than most Eoxians. Apparently, in life, Waneda was obsessed with Eoxian history and the cataclysm that prompted most of the planet's population to turn to undeath. Waneda became intent on achieving immortality with the Eoxians' help. She succeeded, but she spent all of her wealth on the processes and treatments required to achieve her transformation into a ghoul. Given her knowledge of Eoxian culture and history, she then sought work with the planet's government. It was Ambassador Gevalarsk Nor himself who offered Waneda a position at the Ministry of Eternal Vigilance."

What is the Ministry of Eternal Vigilance? "The Ministry of Eternal Vigilance is a bureaucratic branch of the Eoxian government—though a very small branch, to be honest. Eoxian law requires citizens to report all Corpse Fleet activity they witness or suspect. The ministry takes these reports and provides copies to interested parties as necessary—law enforcement agencies, the Eoxian embassy on Absalom Station, or the Stewards. In fact, Eox's ambassadors and government officials make a dutiful show of regularly handing over all of the ministry's reports to the Stewards. It's very important that the Pact Worlds know that the Eoxians are making every possible effort to disavow and eliminate the Corpse Fleet. It's a very thorough system designed to ease the fears of other Pact Worlds members and help Eox avoid blame for the Corpse Fleet's actions.

"Of course, in practice, the system is not so smooth. The Eoxians file precious few reports about the Corpse Fleet, given the planet's population. Some say there are a significant number of Corpse Fleet sympathizers among the residents of Eox's Necropoleis as well as among the bone sages who rule the planet."

What exactly is Waneda's job? "Waneda Trux is the director—and only full-time employee—of the Ministry of Eternal Vigilance. All reports of Corpse Fleet activity on Eox cross her desk, at least officially, and her office keeps files on every reported incident. Unfortunately, there are also reports of Eoxian citizens who provide real information about the Corpse Fleet being intimidated or even attacked by Corpse Fleet sympathizers who believe elebrians should not betray their own kind. This surely does not make Waneda's job any easier.

"Given the supposed ambivalence that many Eoxians exhibit toward the Corpse Fleet, it is perhaps no surprise that Ambassador Nor installed a non-elebrian in this post. A human ghoul would likely be less intimidating than a powerful necrovite, and thus more likely to receive reports from citizens. In addition, a former human would have no sympathy for the Corpse Fleet, as an elebrian or other native Eoxian might. The last impression Ambassador Nor wants to give the Pact Worlds is that Eox is not taking the Corpse Fleet threat seriously."

Will Waneda help us find the Corpse Fleet? "No, I do not believe so. Her job is strictly to take reports from Eoxian citizens regarding the Corpse Fleet. She's not a law enforcement agent, and her superiors do not want her or her ministry to get personally involved in such situations. However, she should be able to give you the most up-to-date leads about the Corpse Fleet's activities on Eox."

Is Eox safe for us? "Certainly—quite safe! All of Orphys is contained beneath an atmosphere dome, so even living creatures can venture about without taking personal environmental protection measures. Waneda Trux has agreed to allow you the use of an empty office in the headquarters of the Ministry of Eternal Vigilance.

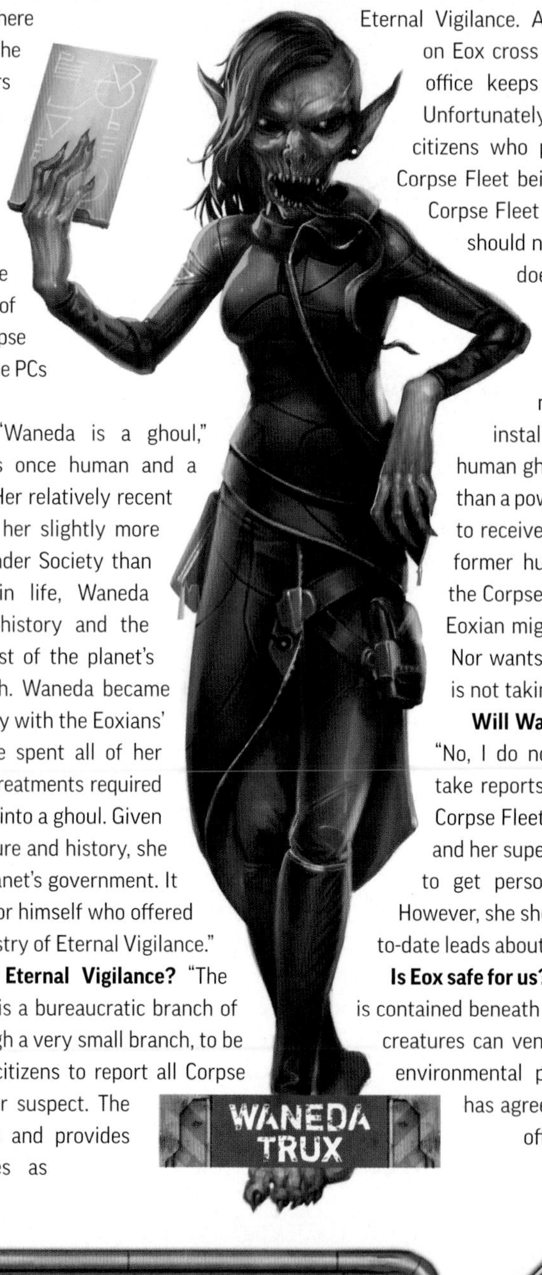

WANEDA TRUX

The local authorities know that you are coming and that you are Starfinders on official business, so you should not have any official interference. On the other hand, I hear that many of Eox's undead citizens can be downright rude to the living, so you would be wise to be prepared for anything. But Eox is otherwise quite safe, I assure you!"

Treasure: Although the PCs did not actually find the Devourer cult in the Diaspora, they did discover and explore the cultists' hidden base, and Chiskisk informs the PCs that the Starfinder Society has procured the payment they were promised, though the expectation is that the PCs will continue their search for the cult. For their efforts in the Star-Eater's Spine, the PCs each receive 2,500 credits transferred to their respective bank accounts. In addition, Chiskisk promises a similar reward if the PCs' mission on Eox is successful (see Concluding the Adventure for details).

THE CORPSE FLEET'S MACHINATIONS

Although the PCs don't know it, the Corpse Fleet is more than one step ahead of them in tracking the Cult of the Devourer and potentially finding the Stellar Degenerator. In fact, the Corpse Fleet is fully aware that the PCs are on its trail and has put plans into motion to stop them, even before the PCs land on Eox. Following the PCs' discovery of Commander Hebiza Eskolar aboard the quarantined mining ship *Acreon* (see *Starfinder Adventure Path* #1), the Corpse Fleet's leaders initially assumed the PCs were merely a loose end, but the actions of the PCs since then have convinced the Corpse Fleet to eliminate the PCs for good.

At this point, the Corpse Fleet is aware that the PCs escaped their ambush in the Diaspora, but they also know there's no chance the PCs will follow them immediately to Nejeor, given that they erased that piece of data entirely from the Devourer cult's datacore. The Corpse Fleet now assumes that the PCs are coming to Eox to search for more clues, especially since their spies on Absalom Station have confirmed that the Starfinder Society's Chiskisk has recently met with Ambassador Gevalarsk Nor multiple times to discuss the situation.

As a result, the Corpse Fleet has seized the opportunity to set a clever trap for the PCs by sending instructions to one of their agents on Eox. Zeera Vesh is a jiang-shi vampire and a newly minted captain in the Corpse Fleet. She works clandestinely on Eox to assess the political situation on the elebrian home world, plant red herrings to throw off the local and intrasystem authorities, and generally advance the Corpse Fleet's agenda as needed. Captain Vesh desperately wants to prove herself invaluable to the Corpse Fleet's high command and land a better assignment offworld. She's been promised exactly that, but only if she can find a way to dispose of the PCs on Eox without raising any red flags with the Ministry of Eternal Vigilance, Eox's diplomatic delegation on Absalom Station, or the Stewards.

To that end, Captain Vesh enlisted the help of Xerantha Mortrant, a reclusive undead creature called a marrowblight who is a strong supporter of the Corpse Fleet. Vesh had already been working on recruiting a disillusioned bone trooper named Harvinne Nessex into the Corpse Fleet; now she's brought Harvinne into the plan as well. With her pawns in place, Vesh has spent the past several days engineering minor events to make it appear that the Corpse Fleet is active in Orphys and ensuring that witnesses report these incidents to the Ministry of Eternal Vigilance. She instructed Harvinne to leave an obvious clue behind that would prompt her flatmate to file a report with the ministry, which would lead the PCs to Xerantha when they inevitably investigated the report. Captain Vesh also stole synthetic flesh from the vats at Fleshworn Fabrications, left an obvious Corpse Fleet badge at the scene of the crime, and sprinkled some of Xerantha's shed osteoderms into the empty vat for good measure. Vesh's hope is that these planted clues will lead the PCs to believe that the Corpse Fleet agents with the information they seek lurk just outside the city. When the PCs leave the safety of the necropolis for the harsh wilds of Eox's surface to investigate, Vesh has directed Xerantha to eliminate them. If that doesn't work, Captain Vesh will confront the PCs and destroy them for good.

ARRIVING ON EOX

The journey from the Diaspora to Eox takes 1d6 days using the Drift or 1d6+2 days using conventional thrusters. Eox is a dead world, with no seas or oceans, and what's left of its thin atmosphere is toxic, radioactive, both, or worse. As the PCs approach the planet, they are contacted by Eoxian Space Defense officials on the ancient orbital defense platform called the Sentinel, who request identification and the PCs' destination. Most interplanetary traffic to and from Eox goes through the domed spaceport called Pact Port, but the PCs' business lies in the necropolis-city of Orphys. Fortunately, Orphys has its own small spaceport, so the PCs are directed there. Once they pass through customs and immigration under the watchful eye sockets of undead officials, the PCs are free to enter the city. The PCs' contact, Waneda Trux, can be found at the Ministry of Eternal Vigilance in a sector of Orphys called the Splice.

THE SPLICE

Orphys is one of Eox's great necropolises, but the Splice is one of the city's most unappealing districts. Largely industrial and utilitarian, the Splice is home to several necrograft factories, which lay the unpleasant reality of this technology's fabrication bare. These factories are large, dirty, and unsightly. Most of the fusion of undead flesh and technology required to create necrografts takes place inside the factories, but other rather morbid processes also happen on these facilities' open-air grounds. This includes the cultivation of massive amounts of vat-grown, genetically synthesized living flesh as well as the transportation of this unpleasant crop via flesh elevators up into the factories.

Beyond the necrograft factories, the Splice is also home to rows of slum-like abodes where some of Orphys's poorest and politically disfavored citizens live, including those few living species who have agreed to work for the Eoxians—often in the nearby necrograft factories—in exchange for the gift of undeath once their mortal forms have weakened. Of course, where there's a population, there are also businesses to serve the residents, and the Splice is no different. However, local law enforcement rarely turns its attention toward the hardscrabble district, so many of the Splice's business proprietors are shady, even by Eoxian standards. Visitors are uncommon in the Splice, and amenities for the living are scarce enough to be nearly nonexistent.

In this part of the adventure, the PCs' activities are mostly confined to the Splice—specifically that portion detailed in the map on page 26. If the PCs wish to purchase or upgrade gear, or even partake of some of Eox's grisly necrograft technology, there are shops located quite near the Ministry of Eternal Vigilance that they can visit (see areas **D** and **E**). If you wish to further detail Orphys or other regions of Eox, using the information in the Eox gazetteer on pages 36–41 as a foundation, you can certainly allow the PCs to explore farther afield, though such endeavors are outside the scope of this adventure. Of course, if the PCs spend too much time off-task, Chiskisk might contact them to remind them that the clock is ticking on their mission, as both the Cult of the Devourer and the Corpse Fleet are ahead of them.

While the PCs are adventuring on Eox, it's important to keep a couple of key environmental concerns in mind. The first is Eox's "local day," which is as long as 30 Pact Standard days (or 720 Pact Standard hours). Like the rest of the Pact Worlds, Eox defaults to the 24-hour Pact Standard day, which makes timekeeping easy and universal, but for the likely duration of the PCs' stay, Eox will be in its 15-day-long night, which means darkness or dim light anywhere that doesn't have artificial illumination.

In addition, Orphys is one of the planet's major necropolises, and it's a hub for living visitors to Eox—though a relatively meager one, given the circumstances. As such, the entire city is covered in a carefully engineered protective dome that contains a breathable atmosphere for living creatures. The PCs can thus move around Orphys without worrying about using their armor's environmental protections. However, the dome's protection does not extend to areas outside the city's limits. The atmosphere in these locales (including areas **H** and **I**, where the PCs must eventually venture) is thin and toxic (*Starfinder Core Rulebook* 396).

C. MINISTRY OF ETERNAL VIGILANCE

A wide, two-story building of black and rust-dappled gray stands out from the other dilapidated structures on this densely packed block. A holographic banner above the sliding double entryway displays the words "Ministry of Eternal Vigilance" in Common and Eoxian. A smaller sign on the front doors declares that the office is open for at least 12 hours every Pact Standard day, even if the stench from the nearby necrograft factory and the building's lack of windows and architectural accouterments are less than inviting.

The Ministry of Eternal Vigilance sits on Carpalspur Street, nestled between necrograft factories and shops. Compared with other government buildings elsewhere in Orphys, the ministry is remote, run down, and politically ignored for the most part. Inside, the office is rather dull and sterile. The ministry building has two floors, briefly detailed below.

C1. Lobby: The ministry's ground floor contains a large waiting room with rows of rusty and, in some cases, lopsided hover chairs. A tall, boxy machine in a corner dispenses numbered tokens. Beside the machine, projected in a hologram on the wall, are instructions for reporting Corpse Fleet activity to the ministry. A wide front desk with a teller-like window faces the lobby at one end, with a holographic numerical display. Behind the front desk, stairs lead to the second floor, though they are roped off with industrial-grade silver tape labeled "No Public Access."

C2. Living Quarters: The building's upper floor houses the personal quarters of the ministry's director, Waneda Trux—government housing is a part of her compensation for the job—and several supply and storage rooms. One of these supply rooms has been cleared to accommodate the PCs, and grimy impressions on the floor show where filing cabinets and office furniture once stood. Now, the room holds a number of thin foam sleeping pads equal to the number of PCs. These, plus a small connected washroom with a deep sink, round out the amenities that Waneda felt obligated to supply her visitors.

Creatures: The first time the PCs visit the Ministry (assuming it's during business hours), there are only two people present: a shabby human man sitting in the lobby, and a female ghoul sitting behind the front desk, absently entering information from an enormous stack of papers into a computer terminal sitting on the desk. The human man is **Shan Goulding** (N male human), a worker in a nearby necrograft factory. The ghoul bureaucrat is **Waneda Trux** (LN female human ghoul), Director of the Ministry of Eternal Vigilance and its only full-time employee.

According to the holographic instructions in the lobby, visitors should take a numbered token from the machine in the corner and have a seat. When their number is called, they should check in at the front desk, where a ministry official will assist them. The PCs can choose to take a number as described above and wait in the lobby until their number is called. If they wish to interact with Shan Goulding, see The Waiting Room below.

Alternatively, the PCs can simply walk right up to the front desk and attempt to engage with Waneda Trux directly. Like government bureaucrats throughout the Pact Worlds, Waneda ignores anyone who does not follow the posted instructions, but as soon as the PCs identify themselves as Starfinders, that Chiskisk sent them, or that they are investigating the Corpse Fleet, Waneda finally acknowledges their presence. See Meeting the Director below for details on the PCs' interactions with Waneda.

The Waiting Room

The human Shan Goulding is waiting in the lobby to file a report on Corpse Fleet activity. Although Shan is not a significant part of the adventure's plot, PCs who talk to him can gain a small boon that will help them when they later visit area **G**.

Shan works at the nearby Fleshworn Fabrications necrograft factory (area **G**) as a line inspector, examining cured pieces of vat-grown flesh to ensure that they fit the specific sizes and shapes needed for creating ocular necrografts. He was hired by a bone sage who is partial owner of the factory; once Shan completes 3 more Eoxian years (15 Pact Standard years) of service, the bone sage has promised him the gift of immortality as an undead ghoul.

Shan is locked in a bitter feud with a half-elf line inspector named Frenzel, and he is planning to report his rival for secretly being a Corpse Fleet agent. Shan's story is a lie, and it can be recognized as such with a successful DC 19 Sense Motive check to detect deception, but if the PCs commiserate with Shan and succeed at a DC 18 Diplomacy check to change Shan's attitude to friendly (his initial attitude is indifferent), he reveals that a flesh brewer at the factory, a corpsefolk—an undead zombie that retains its intelligence and personality—named Voxel also hates Frenzel. Shan further explains that, if the PCs ever need anything from the factory, they should talk to Voxel and tell him Shan sent them. Mentioning Shan's name provides the PCs with a +4 circumstance bonus to all Diplomacy checks they attempt while interacting with Voxel at Fleshworn Fabrications (area **G**).

Allow the PCs to interact with Shan for as long as they like before Waneda calls his number. Shan goes to the front desk, where Waneda listens to his story, jots down a few notes, and then dismisses him. She considers the human's story specious at best and an outright fabrication at worst, and Waneda has no need for a longer, more detailed interview to file an official report. Curiously, there is no penalty for filing a false report at the ministry; the director simply labels such reports "unfounded."

Once she has finished with Shan, Waneda spends a few minutes doing some busy work while pointedly ignoring the PCs. After several long minutes, she finally calls the PCs' number; see Meeting the Director below.

Meeting the Director

Once the PCs have Waneda Trux's attention, the ghoul greets them.

> "Ah. The Starfinders. The bug sent you, huh? You know the stuff people report to me is mostly garbage, right? Petty, stupid complaints about the neighbors or outright lies about rivals and enemies, and none of 'em have nothing to do with the Corpse Fleet.
>
> "Still, once in a thousand moons, we actually get a legitimate lead or two. When that happens, I forward the reports to the government, who passes them on to the authorities and the Pact Council and all the Pact Worlds, or so I'm told. This time, I'm giving 'em to you too. You want to use 'em to go after the Corpse Fleet, be my guest. Literally, since I was instructed to set aside a room upstairs for you. It's yours for as long as you're here, as an office and as a bedroom, since you lot still need sleep, I guess. But don't rush your business on my behalf; I just love strangers—especially living ones I can't eat—staying in my office, particularly when my boss is pretty much forcing me to play host." Waneda smiles disagreeably, revealing sharp, scraggly teeth and a long, curling tongue.

In general, Waneda is an irascible ghoul and a disgruntled and disillusioned bureaucrat. Never a cheerful person in life, her undead transformation did little to change her dour disposition. How helpful she is toward the PCs depends on how cooperative the PCs were with Ambassador Gevalarsk Nor—Waneda's boss—back on Absalom Station.

In *Starfinder Adventure Path* #1, Ambassador Nor asked the PCs to recover a "package" from the quarantined ship *Acreon*—a package that turned out to be a Corpse Fleet officer named Hebiza Eskolar. If the PCs delivered Commander Eskolar to Nor (or they delivered the package without ever discovering Eskolar inside) and parted on good terms with the ambassador, Nor has instructed Waneda to provide the PCs with whatever assistance they require, within the bounds of her position as an Eoxian government employee. In addition, he sent her some files to pass along to the PCs (see below).

On the other hand, if the PCs' relationship with Ambassador Nor did not end well (such as if they handed Commander Eskolar over to the Stewards or station security), then Nor has simply informed Waneda that Starfinders are coming to visit, and it's up to her how to deal with them (with the strong implication that he personally disapproves of them). In this case, Waneda gives her natural ill temper full rein, and the PCs must convince her to assist them. Waneda's initial attitude is unfriendly, and the PCs must succeed at a DC 21

Diplomacy check to change her attitude to make her at least indifferent to them before she agrees to help. Alternatively, the PC can attempt a DC 16 Intimidate check to bully Waneda into helping them, though this will do little to endear the ghoul to them.

Assuming the PCs are on relatively good terms with Waneda (or have at least convinced her to provide the minimum necessary assistance), she has the following information to relay regarding recent Corpse Fleet activity.

"I've got two reports that came in during the last week," Waneda explains. "They're the only ones with any merit at all recently, to be honest with you. The authorities might get to investigating 'em soon, but I'm willing to bet your business is more urgent."

Waneda shows the PCs the two incident reports on her computer screen (see **Handout #1** and **Handout #2** on page 25); she can also transmit copies of the files to the PCs' computers, if desired.

"You should probably look into both of these as soon as you can. The flesh brewer works at Fleshworn Fabrications. He said to ask for him at the factory's back gates, which are right across the street from the ministry. That delightful stench you smell is from the flesh vats in the factory yard. I suppose you don't like it much but it just makes me hungry. The retired trooper lives down the way. She's retired, so she should be available whenever—what else is she going to do? If there's anything else, I guess you can ask me."

At this point, if the PCs are on good terms with Gevalarsk Nor, Waneda informs them that the ambassador has compiled a dossier of known Corpse Fleet agents currently active on Eox. "I don't how this background material will help you, but Ambassador Nor insisted you have it," Waneda says as she passes it along to the PCs. The information in the dossier is difficult to parse without much context, but it does include the names of the following Corpse Fleet agents: Rialphus Evanko, Zeera Vesh, and Woan Watten. Two of these names are red herrings; the third (Zeera Vesh) is the name of the Corpse Fleet agent that the PCs will confront at the end of the adventure. There is little the PCs can do with any of this information at this point, but reading through the dossier can give the PCs some key information for their final battle (see area **I** for more information).

The PCs might have some questions for Waneda about topics beyond recent Corpse Fleet activity. Her answers to some likely PC questions are provided below.

How did you come to work at the Ministry of Eternal Vigilance? "Gevalarsk Nor offered me the job a year ago, and I needed it. Indentured servitude for undeath is a scam. I didn't want to work my skin off for some bone sage until I was old and my body broke, so I spent my life savings to come to Eox and wrangle the science I needed to become a ghoul now. And isn't the result gorgeous?" Waneda sarcastically strikes a pose.

"Anyway, my transformation completely cleaned me out, so I needed a paying gig. Ambassador Nor was familiar with my research and writings on Eoxian history and thought I'd be a good fit for this 'glamorous' post. Said I'd get free housing and all the spare time I wanted to pursue my research. Well, half of that was true. I got a place to live—upstairs, which means I almost never get to leave the office—but I don't have time for anything beyond the job. Folks come in here with every complaint you can imagine: 'My neighbor kicked my pet skullcrab; I think she's a Corpse Fleet sympathizer' and 'The Corpse Fleet stole the brand-new bone fountain from my front yard.' Never ends. Bunch of garbage."

What does your work entail? "A citizen comes in and takes a number. When I call the number, they come up to the front desk here. I give 'em a short form and ask 'em a few preliminary questions. If it seems like their story has some merit, I bring 'em back here for a more thorough interview, and I generate a more detailed long-form report. Those are the reports I send on up the chain. This happens every day. Over and over. For eternity. Pretty exciting, eh?"

Will you help us track down the Corpse Fleet or its agents? "Nope. Not my job. I just take the reports, file 'em, and send 'em on. You want to take on the Corpse Fleet by yourselves, count me out. I'm just a government employee, and that's way above my pay grade."

Do you have any of the evidence mentioned in the reports? "No. That's for the authorities to worry about. I'm not a cop and I don't make cases against the Corpse Fleet. As far as I know, the citizens who made the reports should still have any evidence mentioned in their reports."

Do you know why a Corpse Fleet officer was being shipped to Ambassador Nor? "Do I look like a foreign service official to you? Look around—if Orphys was a living city, we'd be sitting in its bowels right now. Nor hired me, but I've got nothing to do with ambassadors and diplomats, and I haven't been on Absalom Station since I was alive. If you're really concerned, you can file an incident report with the Ministry of Eternal Vigilance. I'm sure the ambassador will give your report all the attention he lavishes on the others. Ha!"

Beyond answering the above questions, Waneda can also relay any information about her job and background that the PCs didn't get from Chiskisk, as described in the Transmission from Chiskisk section on page 19. The same holds true for any information in the Corpse Fleet sidebar on page 14 that the PCs might have missed, as well as the information on the Corpse Fleet presented on page 472 of the *Starfinder Core Rulebook*. In addition, as a historian, Waneda can share the details of Eox and its history as found on pages 450–451 of the *Core Rulebook*. If the PCs ask Waneda about the local area, she can share the information in the Splice section on page 21.

Treasure: If the PCs are on good terms with Ambassador Nor, Waneda says that the ambassador has instructed her to give the PCs 1,000 credits apiece to purchase supplies to aid

Handout #1

MINISTRY OF ETERNAL VIGILANCE

Corpse Fleet Incident Report

Report Filed By Voxel Darksend
Necrotype/Species Corpsefolk (elebrian)
Address 43 Sethrot Commons, Upper Vamsbank, Orphys
Occupation Flesh brewer
Employer Fleshworn Fabrications
Available for Follow-Up Interview? Yes (at work only)
Filing Date 4 Kuthona 317 AG
Recorded By Waneda Trux, Director

Incident of Suspected Corpse Fleet Activity "Sometime between the hours of 11:30 and 13:00 yesterday (3 Kuthona), an entire vat of flesh disappeared from FWF's flesh yards. Upon discovering the flesh was missing, I found a badge with the Corpse Fleet's insignia next to the empty vat. I also recorded a digital photo of the badge's location. It seems pretty obvious to me that the Corpse Fleet stole the vat flesh for some unknown purpose."

Handout #2

MINISTRY OF ETERNAL VIGILANCE

Corpse Fleet Incident Report

Report Filed By Gretal Rapinder
Necrotype/Species Bone trooper (elebrian)
Address 5236 Bareknuckle Way, Splice, Orphys
Occupation Navy trooper (retired)
Employer 5th Squadron, Eoxian Navy
Available for Follow-Up Interview? Yes
Filing Date 6 Kuthona 317 AG
Recorded By Waneda Trux, Director

Incident of Suspected Corpse Fleet Activity "On or around 00:00 on 4 Kuthona, my flatmate, Harvinne Nessex (also a 5th Squadron veteran), left our residence, saying she needed to purchase new outerwear—a curious task, especially considering the late hour. In any case, she never returned to the flat. This morning (6 Kuthona), I entered her quarters and discovered that most of her belongings were gone, but I found a scrap of paper on the floor that looks like it fell out of her journal (Harvinne keeps a real paper diary that she actually writes in with a stylus). On this scrap, Harvinne wrote about her disillusionment with current Eoxian policy and her intention to join a contingent of the Corpse Fleet that is currently operating in Orphys. I believe that Harvinne has left the Splice to enlist in the Corpse Fleet."

them in their mission to track down the Corpse Fleet's agents on Eox. Waneda can point the PCs to nearby shops (areas **D** and **E**) if they are interested.

Development: As mentioned in the description of area **C**, Waneda has set aside a room on the ministry's second floor to house the PCs while they're on Eox. They are under no obligation to take these quarters, though, and can find other lodgings in Orphys at two to three times the prices listed on page 235 of the *Core Rulebook* (most Eoxians are undead, so full amenities for living creatures are at a premium).

Regardless of where the PCs decide to stay, their next task should be to follow up on the leads Waneda has given them. These are all located in the Splice: the retired bone trooper Gretal Rapinder can be found in area **F**, while the flesh brewer Voxel Darksend works in area **G**. In addition to these encounter locations, two other sites are detailed below (areas **D** and **E**). While not directly related to the adventure's plot, they do provide some local flavor and give the PCs the chance to purchase additional gear. The PCs can visit these locations in any order they wish. Lastly, the PCs' investigations will trigger another encounter that is not tied to a specific location; see **Event 3** for details on when this encounter occurs.

D. GENTLESAGE'S NECROGRAFTS & SUNDRIES

Bright tubes of neon pinks, greens, and blues form a large sign outside of this rusty storefront. "Gentlesage's Necrografts & Sundries," it reads in a swooping font reminiscent of handwriting. Fluorescent paint finishes the display with an image of a rotting undead humanoid in a deeply cut chiffon shirt, revealing a vestigial undead head protruding from one shoulder. Both heads are wearing top hats and monocles.

It's clear that the owner of this business has gone to great lengths to build a brand that's refined and has the veneer of luxury, even if it is located in a seedy part of the city. The store's inventory, consisting mostly of necrografts but also including a few biotech items, is displayed on plush pillows and within curtained shadow boxes.

Creature: The shop's proprietor stands behind the cheaply gilded counter inside. **Jonesworth Lengfoll** (N male corpsefolk)—who calls himself the Gentlesage—is a corpsefolk, a decaying undead zombie that retains its intelligence and personality. The Gentlesage is dressed in a cobbled-together sort of archaic finery, with a patchwork tailed coat, a dingy top hat, a dented monocle, and a gold-colored cane covered in greenish patina. A small vestigial head on the Gentlesage's shoulder protrudes from his ruffled shirt, just like the sign outside. Jonesworth thinks himself rather stately and wishes to exude such an air for his customers, thinking that most will believe it impressive, but his affectation is mostly a way to feel superior to the other creatures in the Splice.

Jonesworth has been a corpsefolk for nearly a century and largely dislikes living creatures, and his initial attitude toward the PCs is unfriendly. When he sees the PCs, the Gentlesage eyes them warily but nonetheless offers a greeting that he surely believes to be refined. "Ah, customers who bear the spark of life," he says. "You are most welcome at Gentlesage's Necrografts and Sundries, but do know that I will not tolerate breathing on my wares. It conveys the stench of the living, don't you know, which is most off-putting for my normal clientele. You understand, I'm sure."

Despite his attitude, the Gentlesage will sell the PCs any necrograft (see page 42) with an item level of 8th or lower. Additionally, there is a 50% chance that the Gentlesage has any biotech item (*Core Rulebook* pages 211–212) of item level 8th or lower in stock and available for sale. Should the PCs inquire, the Gentlesage's vestigial head (whom he refers to as "my personal assistant") is a custom necrograft crafted specifically for him, and it is not for sale.

Development: If the PCs improve the Gentlesage's attitude to friendly or better with a successful DC 29 Diplomacy check to change his attitude, he warns them about roving gangs of ghouls that have been prowling the Splice recently in search of what they call "traitors;" Jonesworth guesses this means anyone who is indifferent to the idea of Eoxian superiority, including those who would report Corpse Fleet activity, but likely includes the living—such as the PCs—as well. This foreshadows the encounter the PCs will face in area **F**.

THE BUSINESS OF NECROGRAFTS

Besides being infamous for its almost entirely undead population, Eox is also well known among the Pact Worlds for its pioneering of necrografts. Neither cybernetic nor biotech, necrografts are augmentations crafted from undead tissue. Necrografts can be implanted into an individual's body to enhance it in some way, whether to restore lost functionality due to illness or injury, augment natural systems, or provide a magical boost to the user's abilities. The selling and installation of necrografts account for a large percentage of the economy of Orphys, and the seeking of necrografts is one of the primary reasons a living creature might visit the undead planet. The business of necrografts is booming on Eox and in Orphys in particular, where enormous factories churn out this technology practically day and night. For more information about specific necrografts that players might want to purchase, see page 42.

E. BONESMITH'S BOUTIQUE

Windows covered with mealy boards and one lopsided automatic door adorn the outside of this dingy one-story building. Above the entrance is a hologram of a bizarre, ostentatious hat made entirely of tiny bones and the words "Bonesmith's Boutique: Merchandise You Can Trust!"

This rather disreputable business sells a motley assortment of weapons, armor, and sundry supplies.

Creature: The boutique is named for its proprietor and sole employee, **Bonesmith Jaklyn** (CN female bone trooper). If the PCs walk inside, Jaklyn is behind the front desk wearing an elaborate pirate-style outfit and the same strange hat depicted on the sign outside. When the bone trooper sees the PCs, she opens her mouth wide (the skeletal equivalent of a smile), revealing several golden teeth. "Ah, breathers!" Jaklyn exclaims, using a common Eoxian term for living individuals. "Welcome to Bonesmith Jaklyn's boutique! We've got everything your little beating hearts might desire—and probably more!"

There is an 80% chance that Bonesmith's Boutique has in stock any weapon or suit of armor of item level 8th or lower, as well as the same chance of having any drugs, medicinals, poisons, or magic serums of item level 8th or lower. Despite her overly friendly greeting, however, Bonesmith Jaklyn is a con artist and a lout, and she particularly enjoys overcharging living customers for her wares. If the PCs make no attempt to engage Jaklyn in conversation, she charges 20% above normal prices for her in-stock items. However, if the PCs share any gossip with her, or if they spend any time complimenting her hat, her outfit, her teeth, or the like, she sells items to the PCs at their normal prices. If the PCs really lay on the compliments and one them succeeds at a DC 18 Bluff or Diplomacy check, Bonesmith Jaklyn offers them a storewide 10% discount. Further, if Jaklyn's attitude toward them is friendly or better and the PCs later need to flee from the ghoul soldiers in area **F** (or any other enemies they might make in this area), the bone trooper can gladly provide them with a good hiding spot in the back of her store.

F. PENSIONER'S FLAT (CR 7)

The narrow sliding door to this residential building bears the tarnished metal numbers "5236," with the final digit drooping to the side. The door is slightly dented and hangs partially open.

This is the home of Gretal Rapinder and Harvinne Nessex, two retired bone troopers who formerly served in the 5th Squadron of the Eoxian Navy. The door to the flat has indeed been forced open, as a successful DC 10 Engineering check to assess stability reveals. The sound of rasping voices shouting angry taunts can clearly be heard coming from inside the residence.

Creatures: Harvinne is still missing (see area **I**), but **Gretal Rapinder** (LN female bone trooper) is home. Unfortunately, word that Gretal reported Harvinne to the Ministry of Eternal

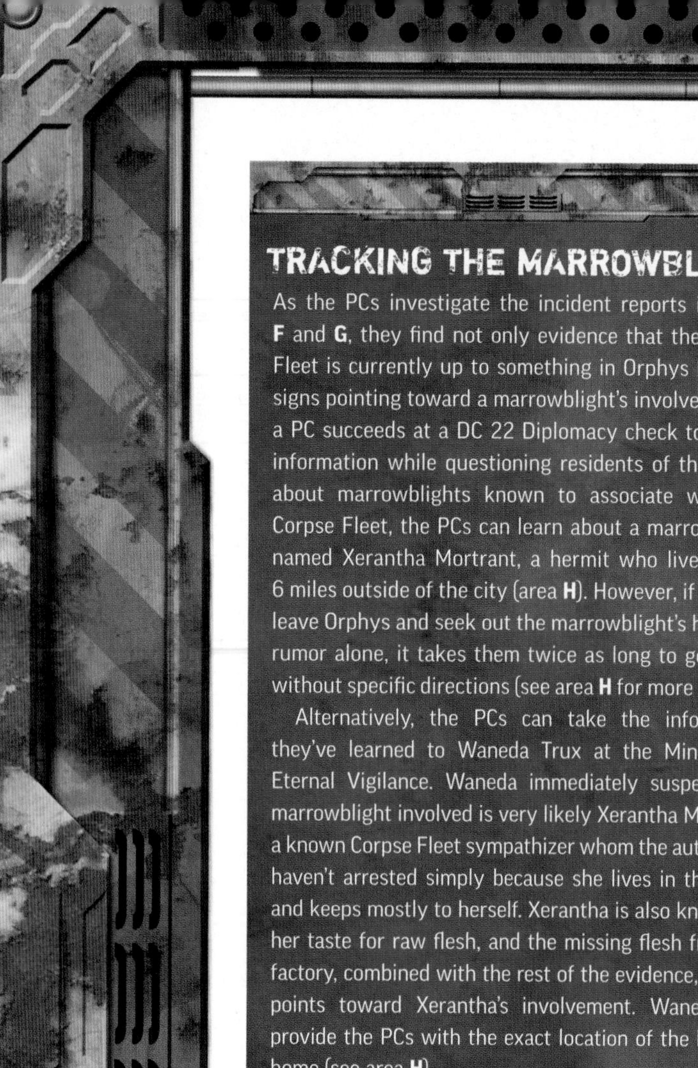

TRACKING THE MARROWBLIGHT

As the PCs investigate the incident reports in areas **F** and **G**, they find not only evidence that the Corpse Fleet is currently up to something in Orphys but also signs pointing toward a marrowblight's involvement. If a PC succeeds at a DC 22 Diplomacy check to gather information while questioning residents of the Splice about marrowblights known to associate with the Corpse Fleet, the PCs can learn about a marrowblight named Xerantha Mortrant, a hermit who lives about 6 miles outside of the city (area **H**). However, if the PCs leave Orphys and seek out the marrowblight's home on rumor alone, it takes them twice as long to get there without specific directions (see area **H** for more details).

Alternatively, the PCs can take the information they've learned to Waneda Trux at the Ministry of Eternal Vigilance. Waneda immediately suspects the marrowblight involved is very likely Xerantha Mortrant, a known Corpse Fleet sympathizer whom the authorities haven't arrested simply because she lives in the wilds and keeps mostly to herself. Xerantha is also known for her taste for raw flesh, and the missing flesh from the factory, combined with the rest of the evidence, further points toward Xerantha's involvement. Waneda can provide the PCs with the exact location of the hermit's home (see area **H**).

Vigilance for potential ties to the Corpse Fleet has reached the 5th Squadron, and a few of its current members who believe deeply in Eoxian superiority have taken leave from the navy to harass those they consider "traitors to Eox." Three ghoul soldiers—Danine, Larex, and Welles—have taken offense with Gretal's execution of her legally obligated reporting duties, and they have come to her flat to teach the retired bone trooper "proper respect" for her home world.

When the PCs arrive, the three ghouls turn on the intruders—these undead nationalists are more than happy to take out their anger and frustrations on the living. During the battle, Gretal tries to stay out of the way. If necessary, you can use the bone trooper stat block on page 56 of *Starfinder Adventure Path* #1 for Gretal, though she is not intended to be a combatant in this encounter.

DANINE, LAREX, AND WELLES (3) — CR 4

XP 1,200 each

Elebrian ghoul soldier (see page 54)

CE Medium undead

Init +7; **Senses** darkvision 60 ft.; **Perception** +10

DEFENSE — **HP** 60 EACH

EAC 16; **KAC** 18

Fort +6; **Ref** +4; **Will** +7

Immunities undead immunities

OFFENSE

Speed 35 ft.

Melee tactical swoop hammer +12 (1d10+9 B; critical knockdown) or

bite +12 (1d6+9 P plus ghoul fever [DC 15] and paralysis [DC 15]) or

claw +12 (1d6+9 S plus paralysis [DC 15])

Ranged frostbite-class zero rifle +9 (1d8+4 C; critical staggered [DC 13]) or

frag grenade II +9 (explode [15 ft., 2d6 P, DC 13])

Space 5 ft.; **Reach** 5 ft. (10 ft. with swoop hammer)

Offensive Abilities fighting style (blitz)

TACTICS

During Combat The ghouls prefer melee combat, and against living opponents, they relish using their natural bite and claw attacks. The ghouls use their swoop hammers against especially dangerous opponents, or switch to their zero rifles to fight foes at range.

Morale The ghouls fight until one has fewer than 10 Hit Points remaining, at which point all three try to flee or, failing that, surrender (the ghouls wanted only to intimidate those they consider "enemies of the state" and weren't planning on actually getting into a life-or-death battle).

STATISTICS

Str +5; **Dex** +3; **Con** –; **Int** +0; **Wis** +0; **Cha** +1

Skills Athletics +15, Intimidate +10, Stealth +10

Languages Common, Eoxian

Other Abilities unliving

Gear officer ceremonial plate, frostbite-class zero rifle with high-capacity battery (40 charges), tactical swoop hammer, frag grenades II (2)

Development: If the PCs defeat the ghouls or drive them away, Gretal expresses her thanks for their help. The bone trooper is concerned about brewing Corpse Fleet activity in the area. She's also a little shaken in the knowledge that her trip to the Ministry of Eternal Vigilance has become public knowledge and that soldiers in her former squadron have taken such offense to her report. A loyal citizen, Gretal simply wants to do right by her planet's legitimate government and military, which required her to report her suspicions about Harvinne.

Although Gretal's appearance is rather unsettling, she is relatively friendly toward the PCs. Without much prompting, Gretal unlocks her flatmate's bedroom (she long ago figured out its passcode) and gives the PCs the journal page she mentioned in her Ministry incident report. The bedroom contains no additional clues, but upon examining the journal scrap, the PCs learn that Harvinne planned to meet with something called "the marrowblight" before taking up her illicit commission in the Corpse Fleet. The PCs can recall that a marrowblight is a type of powerful undead creature with a successful DC 20 Mysticism check. Gretal has not heard of a prominent marrowblight that is locally associated with the Corpse Fleet, however (see the Tracking the Marrowblight sidebar on page 28 for more information).

In gratitude for their help, and also to help the PCs in their future endeavors, Gretal gives the PCs a *haste circuit* armor upgrade from her time in the 5th Squadron. "I was hanging on to this as a souvenir of my time in the service," Gretal says. "Honestly, though, I have no use for it anymore, and it will likely help you more than it would ever help me. But let it be a reminder—not all of us who're dead are bad!"

If the PCs do not intervene, Gretal escapes from the ghouls out the back door. The disgruntled soldiers smash a few things in the flat before leaving the area. If the PCs search Gretal's flat after they leave, they find the door to Harvinne's bedroom locked (hardness 8, HP 30, break DC 24, Engineering DC 25 to disable). Once inside the room, the PCs can easily find the scrap from Harvinne's journal mentioned in Gretal's incident report.

G. FLESHWORN FABRICATIONS

Tall metal walls behind a chain-link fence and wide, looming security gates mark this as some sort of industrial facility. Inside the gates is a massive metal-and-concrete platform resting at the bottom of an enormous elevator shaft. The edges of circular pools or vats containing some strange undulating substance are barely visible behind the fence, sunk deeply in the ground. A sign that reads, "Attention visitors: Call for agent," hangs above an intercom on one side of the gates.

Fleshworn Fabrications manufactures necrografts for various bodily systems and exports them throughout the Pact Worlds. This is the entry to the factory's flesh yards, where the synthetic flesh required for constructing necrografts is created. Essentially, basic biological materials are combined in the yard's large vats and periodically agitated, which leads to the eventual creation of a synthetic substance that looks and functions almost identically to natural tissue. The factory's flesh brewers tend to the vats while batches of flesh are percolating. When each batch has sufficiently matured, the flesh brewers use equipment housed in two large sheds to extract flesh from the vats, transport it to the yard's enormous industrial flesh elevator, and convey it to the curing kilns in the factory's upper reaches. There, other workers cure the flesh until it takes on the characteristics and structure of undead tissue. The cured flesh is then moved to the factory's production lines, where it is cut and shaped or molded into undead organs in preparation for the final necromantic rituals that will transform the inert tissue into proper necrografts. Any PC can recall this information with a successful DC 15 Mysticism check. For more on necrografts, see the Business of Necrografts sidebar on page 27 and page 42 of the Eox gazetteer.

The factory's rear gates are locked (hardness 20, HP 60, break DC 28, Engineering DC 30 to disable) and are likely difficult for the PCs to bypass, but they can use the intercom next to the gates to alert workers inside to their presence. Climbing or flying over the fence and walls is possible, of course, but motion sensors set off an alarm throughout the factory if anyone attempts to bypass the gates in this manner.

Creature: Assuming the PCs visit the factory during normal business hours (06:00 to 18:00 each day), a booming voice answers their call on the intercom (no one answers if

GHOUL SOLDIER

they use the intercom after hours). This is **Voxel Darksend** (N male corpsefolk), the flesh brewer who reported the yard's missing flesh to the Ministry of Eternal Vigilance. Once the PCs identify themselves, Voxel hurries over to open the gates, saying, "Finally! It's about time the Ministry sent somebody! You have no idea how much I've needed you to tell my bosses that I didn't steal or lose the missing flesh. Well? What are you waiting for? Get in here!"

Voxel is fairly coarse and abrupt, but he is not naturally cruel, and he indeed simply wants the PCs to prove that the missing flesh was stolen. Voxel doesn't care much about bureaucracy or the political arrangements between Eox and the Pact Worlds regarding tracking the Corpse Fleet. He assumes that the authorities sent the PCs, and insists on calling them "cops" or "agents," even if the PCs try to correct his assumptions.

As soon as the PCs walk into the flesh yard, Voxel insists on showing them the relevant vat, which is still empty from the recent theft. He also shows the PCs a photo on his datapad of the badge he found next to the vat immediately following the theft's discovery and produces the badge itself. The PCs can confirm that the badge displays the insignia of the Corpse Fleet with a successful DC 20 Culture check.

Voxel certainly seems to be telling the truth about his report and shows concern about the Corpse Fleet's machinations, but if the PCs ask to investigate the site of the theft further, Voxel balks, citing safety regulations and despotic supervisors. If the PCs succeed at a DC 16 Diplomacy check to change Voxel's attitude from indifferent to friendly or better (they gain a +4 circumstance bonus to this check if they mention Shan from the ministry's waiting room in area **C**), Voxel tells the PCs he would let them climb down into the vat but the computer controlling the vat's mechanisms has been malfunctioning for a couple of weeks, making the vat unsafe. The PCs must attempt either a DC 25 Computers check to repair the computer's control module or a DC 20 Engineering check to repair item to fix the mechanism. With a successful check, the PCs repair the vat's controls, enabling them to easily climb down to the bottom of the vat. A PC who succeeds at a DC 15 Perception check while searching the bottom of the vat finds some curious bone spur-like shards among the scraps of synthetic flesh left in the vat. A successful DC 20 Mysticism check reveals that these bony spurs are osteoderms shed by a marrowblight, a type of undead creature.

Treasure: If the PCs promise to give Voxel a signed affidavit that he can show his superiors stating that they have confirmed that the Corpse Fleet was responsible for the missing flesh, the corpsefolk gives them three frag grenades III from his personal stash, which he occasionally uses to dislodge chunks of flesh from the vats (though this is strictly against company policy).

Development: Voxel doesn't know much about marrowblights, nor why one would be interested in the factory's flesh. If the PCs are unable to identify the osteoderms and show them to Waneda, the ministry director immediately recognizes them (see the Tracking the Marrowblight sidebar on page 28 for more information).

Story Award: If the PCs find the marrowblight osteoderms in the empty flesh vat, award them 2,400 XP.

EVENT 3: TYING UP LOOSE ENDS (CR 7)

This encounter occurs while the PCs are in the Splice, investigating the Corpse Fleet incident reports from the Ministry of Eternal Vigilance. It can happen at any point, most likely when the PCs have left an encounter location (such as the Ministry or Fleshworn Fabrications) or are traveling between locations, but its exact timing requires some planning, as the PCs may get a warning beforehand (see below).

As the PCs investigate the Corpse Fleet's activities in the Splice, a faction within the Eoxian government with close ties to the exiled navy decides that the PCs have become too much of a risk to tolerate any longer. Rather than trust the Corpse Fleet's agents to handle matters, this faction determines to tie up the loose end represented by the PCs by sending its own assassins to eliminate them.

Back on Absalom Station, Ambassador Gevalarsk Nor gets wind of this plan through his numerous Eoxian contacts, but what he does with this information depends on how the PCs left their relationship with him. If the PCs did as Nor asked in *Starfinder Adventure Path* #1 and remain on good terms with him, the ambassador instructs Waneda Trux to alert the PCs about the assassins. In this case, Waneda calls the PCs a few minutes before the encounter occurs to warn them of the impending attack. This warning grants the PCs a +4 circumstance bonus to Perception checks to notice the hidden assassins before they attack. On the other hand, if the PCs are not on good terms with Ambassador Nor, they receive no warning (and no bonuses to skill checks) beforehand.

Creatures: Knowing that the PCs are living creatures, the government conspirators have sent two nihilis to attack the PCs. Risen from those who died from exposure to the airless vacuum of space, the nihilis hate the living with a vengeance and can collapse the lungs of living creatures with their decompression gaze ability, as well as manipulate local gravity. The nihilis conceal themselves alongside a path the PCs are likely to take; any PC who fails a DC 21 Perception check to notice the nihilis cannot act in the subsequent surprise round. The undead fight until destroyed.

NIHILIS (2) — CR 5

XP 1,600 each
HP 72 each (*Starfinder Alien Archive* 82)

Treasure: The nihilis have nothing that identifies them or their employers, but each of them carries a credstick with 2,500 credits—their payment for the job.

H. MARROWBLIGHT'S HERMITAGE

Once the PCs have spent some time investigating the Ministry's reports, they should come to the conclusion that a marrowblight named Xerantha Mortrant is somehow involved in the Corpse Fleet's ongoing plots, and they should know approximately where Xerantha lives (see the Tracking the Marrowblight sidebar on page 28 for more information). Waneda Trux should encourage the PCs to confront the marrowblight if they don't decide to do so on their own.

Traveling to Xerantha's home is more complicated than simply walking there, however, as the reclusive marrowblight lives in the wilds well outside of Orphys's atmosphere dome. As a result, for the remainder of the adventure (assuming the PCs don't return to Orphys), the PCs will be exposed to Eox's thin and toxic atmosphere (*Core Rulebook* 396) and must use the environmental protections of their armor to avoid negative effects.

Furthermore, the stretch of terrain between Orphys and Xerantha's hermitage is disconcerting and difficult to travel, with strange rock formations, deep twisting gullies, and massive fields of bleached bones the norm. Xerantha's home is approximately 6 miles outside of Orphys. If the PCs have learned its exact location from Waneda, it takes them 2 hours to walk there from the Splice. If the PCs are searching for Xerantha's home without learning its exact location, it takes 4 hours instead.

Feel free to be creative describing the strange sights the PCs see during their time in the wilds of Eox's blasted surface. You might consider describing Skullcap Gorge (area **I**) as the PCs pass through it on their way to confront the marrowblight to foreshadow the location of their final showdown with Zeera Vesh, though you can keep the area's layout a surprise, to be revealed only when the Corpse Fleet agent springs her ambush. If the PCs need more experience points, this journey is also a good time for an appropriate random encounter to take place.

Use the inset map on page 26 for the following encounters.

H1. Desiccated Garden (CR 9)

The blasted landscape of a wholly devastated and undead planet gives way slightly to this carefully cultivated area surrounding a dilapidated hut. The displays are almost garden-like in their precise arrangement—thin, pliable bones weave intricate patterns in clumps that might otherwise be living bushes, and flutes of skin and cartilage might be mistaken for flowers were it not for the disturbing shapes and absence of brilliant colors.

This peculiar garden lies outside the home of the marrowblight Xerantha Mortrant.

Creature: Xerantha is hiding in her shack (area **H2**), but her pet ellicoth, Trampleram, considers the garden its personal domain, and attacks all intruders. Trampleram attempts to surprise the PCs by circling around the hut and attacking from the side, but its primary goal to prevent anyone from entering area **H2**.

TRAMPLERAM — CR 9

XP 6,400

Ellicoth (*Starfinder Alien Archive* 48)

HP 145

TACTICS

During Combat Trampleram uses its natural gore attack against opponents until it drops below 100 Hit Points, at which point the ellicoth alternates its gores with its soul drain attack, attempting to regain Hit Points to make up for those it's lost.

Morale Trampleram is a rather thick, stubborn beast and fights until it is destroyed.

Hazard: The dusty ground is largely flat, but those squares on the map containing bone bushes are considered difficult terrain. The bone bushes are about 4-1/2 feet tall and provide cover as low obstacles (*Core Rulebook* 254). In addition, any creature that steps into a bone bush square must succeed at a DC 15 Reflex saving throw or gain the entangled condition. Entangled creatures can free themselves from the bone bushes' grasp by succeeding at a DC 20 Strength check or DC 24 Acrobatics check to escape as a full action.

H2. Skin Shack (CR 7)

This bizarre, circular hovel appears to be made from stretched, cured skin wrapped around a frame of massive bones. A front door hewn from sickly wood stands ever so slightly open.

Creature: This shack is home to Xerantha Mortrant, a marrowblight hermit and violent misanthrope, who particularly loathes living creatures. Xerantha is a Corpse Fleet sympathizer and colluder, and she is a coconspirator with the jiang-shi vampire Zeera Vesh. Before the PCs arrived on Eox, Captain Vesh asked for Xerantha's help in eliminating the PCs. All she would have to do was wait for the PCs to come to her home and then kill the interloping intruders—assistance the evil marrowblight was more than willing to provide.

Xerantha is hiding in the back of her shack, waiting for the right moment to ambush the PCs when they enter through the front door. The marrowblight has attempted to make it appear as if she were not home, but a PC who succeeds at a DC 24 Perception check can hear a faint, infrequent scuffling sound as Xerantha shifts slightly in her cramped hiding place. Once two or more of the PCs have entered the shack, Xerantha emerges from her hiding place in the back room and pounces toward the closest PC.

XERANTHA MORTRANT — CR 7

XP 3,200

Female marrowblight (see page 55)

HP 105

Ranged thunderstrike streetsweeper +12 (1d10+7 So; critical knockdown)

TACTICS

During Combat Xerantha uses the furniture inside her home for partial cover and pounces next to opponents to attack them with her claws and spurs and infect them with red ache. If the fight becomes too cramped inside her shack, Xerantha attempts to move outside to her garden (area **H1**). If she can't pin anyone down in melee combat, or when she's outside, Xerantha fires her streetsweeper at enemies at range.

Morale Xerantha is fiercely loyal to the Corpse Fleet and immensely proud of her undead status and hatred of the living. The more her enemies wound her, the more enraged she becomes. Xerantha tries to surrender only if she loses half of her Hit Points or more in a single round (see Development below). Otherwise, the marrowblight fights until destroyed.

STATISTICS

Gear thunderstrike streetsweeper with 2 high-capacity batteries (40 charges each)

Treasure: Xerantha's shack is fairly threadbare and devoid of any items of obvious value. In fact, the whole place amounts to a collection of junk that is either furniture crafted from preserved organic body parts or mostly worthless trophies from intruders the marrowblight has defeated in recent years. However, if the PCs spend 10 minutes searching the place and succeed at a DC 18 Perception check, they find a sack made from the dried organ of some creature hidden behind one of the load-bearing bones in the building's frame. The sack holds a jumbled stash of more than a dozen credsticks, some bent or bloodstained, taken from Xerantha's slain foes. All together, the credsticks contain a total of 7,080 credits. In addition, the PCs can easily see a datapad with a cracked screen sitting atop a pile of the marrowblight's personal belongings (see Development below).

Development: Xerantha's cracked datapad is a simple tier 1 computer, and bypassing the datapad's password is a fairly simple endeavor, requiring a successful DC 17 Computers check to hack the system or a successful DC 17 Engineering check to physically bypass the password through the datapad's hardware so its contents can be downloaded onto a PC's own device. The datapad reveals that Xerantha has indeed been colluding with the Corpse Fleet for a long time, and it contains detailed notes from the marrowblight's earlier meeting with Captain Zeera Vesh. This enables the PCs to learn Vesh's name and her conspiracy with Xerantha and Harvinne Nessex, as well as the clues she planted for the PCs, as detailed in The Corpse Fleet's Machinations on page 21. However, the datapad does not reveal that Captain Vesh plans to ambush the PCs herself—the PCs will discover that fact for themselves in the next encounter, when they face the jiang-shi in Skullcap Gorge on their way back to Orphys.

If Xerantha surrenders to the PCs and is left to her own devices, the marrowblight discreetly follows them to Skullcap Gorge (area **I**) and joins Captain Vesh in the Corpse Fleet's final attempt to eliminate the PCs.

I. SKULLCAP GORGE (CR 9)

This encounter occurs when the PCs pass through an area called Skullcap Gorge, as they travel back to Orphys from the home of the hermit marrowblight Xerantha Mortrant. Read or paraphrase the following as they enter the canyon.

The desolate Eoxian terrain turns macabre here, as the sloping land descends into a gaping canyon that stretches for dozens of yards. But instead of sheer cliffs of rock, towering piles of bones and skulls of all sizes and shapes form the walls of the gorge. At the ravine's eastern end, a wide pool of bubbling green acid abuts a sheer cliff. Several flat, stepped rocks next to the pool approximate a stairway climbing to the top of the cliff.

Perhaps one of the most disconcerting sights between Orphys and the wild wastes beyond, Skullcap Gorge was once a small elebrian village that instantly became a graveyard when cataclysm struck Eox millennia ago. As the undead survivors tried to rebuild their planet in the aftermath, they gathered all of the village's bones into two large piles. However, the sheer macabre volume of the remains—combined with the harsh landscape and the acid pools that spontaneously arose from the ground in several places—led the elebrians to eventually abandon this endeavor. The place soon became known colloquially as Skullcap Gorge, for obvious reasons, and the canyon has since become a hideaway for criminals and outlaws, including members of the Corpse Fleet from time to time.

The PCs enter Skullcap Gorge from the west. The enormous walls of bone to the north and south are 50 to 60 feet high and require a successful DC 20 Athletics check to climb. A line of rocks separates the bottom of the gorge from the pool of acid; the rocks are difficult terrain, but they are not tall enough to provide any significant cover. The acid pool ranges in depth from about a foot at its western edge to 6 feet at its eastern end. Any creature touching the pool takes 3d6 acid damage per round. Swimming or fully submerged creatures take 20d6 acid damage per round.

The stepped rocks leading up to the top of the cliff to the east are each 2 to 3 feet tall with uneven surfaces, and they are considered difficult terrain. The cliff top is 20 feet above the bottom of the gorge.

Creatures: Corpse Fleet Captain Zeera Vesh has been taking pains to track the PCs since they arrived on Eox and began investigating Waneda Trux's Corpse Fleet incident reports. At this point, she knows that the marrowblight Xerantha Mortrant has failed to kill the heroes, so Captain Vesh has rapidly put her backup plan into place—she will finish the PCs herself, ambushing them as they traipse through Skullcap Gorge on their way back to Orphys. To assist her in this task, Captain Vesh has brought along five Corpse Fleet bone troopers (one of these bone troopers is Harvinne Nessex, the flatmate of Gretal Rapinder from area **F**).

Captain Vesh is crouching down on the rocky stairway that climbs to the top of the cliff at the gorge's eastern end. Once the PCs have entered the gorge, the bone troopers move into place behind them to the west. Vesh reveals herself as soon as the PCs are halfway between the acid pool and the western edge of the map, and calls out to them.

"Petty, foolish, *irritating* Starfinders! All of the effort I spent to weave this deadly trap, and for what? To have you bumble through, unharmed and yet still so ignorant? Allow me to enlighten you. I am Captain Zeera Vesh, esteemed officer of the mighty Corpse Fleet—valiant navy of the *true* Eox—and you will go no farther. You've meddled enough in our plans. Now, I shall succeed where my lackeys have failed. I shall destroy you and bring glory to the Corpse Fleet once and for all!"

At this point, Captain Vesh has worked herself into a rage, and she attacks the PCs without any further delay. If the PCs received Ambassador Nor's dossier of information about active Corpse Fleet agents on Eox from Waneda Trux (see Meeting the Director on page 23), allow them to know up to three useful pieces of information about the jiang-shi, as if they had succeeded at a DC 29 Mysticism skill check to identify creatures.

BONE TROOPERS (5) — CR 3

XP 800 each

Starfinder Adventure Path #1 56

HP 34 each

TACTICS

During Combat The bone troopers position themselves to pin opponents between themselves and Captain Vesh. The troopers cast *supercharge weapon* on their pistols before attacking, and they launch *magic missiles* at enemies with concealment or behind cover.

Morale Fanatically loyal to the Corpse Fleet, the bone troopers fight until destroyed.

ZEERA VESH — CR 6

XP 2,400

Female elebrian jiang-shi operative (see page 58)

HP 80

TACTICS

During Combat Captain Vesh targets foes with her shirren-eye rifle, using her debilitating sniper exploit to make them flat-footed or off-target, as the situation requires. Vesh's hopping gait allows her to traverse the rocky stairs at full speed, so she tries to lure as many opponents onto the stairs as possible to take advantage of their hindered movement. Vesh tries to stay just out of melee reach, slowly moving toward the top of the stairs as needed. Once on top of the cliff, Vesh attacks with her claws, attempting to grapple her enemies and drain their chi or bull rush them off the cliff and into the acid pool below.

Morale Captain Vesh fights until destroyed.

STATISTICS

Gear freebooter armor II (mk 1 electrostatic field), advanced shirren-eye rifle with 25 sniper rounds, corona laser pistol with 2 batteries (20 charges each), secure data module (see Development below), credstick (4,000 credits)

Development: If the PCs manage to subdue Captain Vesh without destroying her, she refuses to tell them anything about the Corpse Fleet's plans, their recent activities in the Diaspora, their current location, or their plans for the Stellar Degenerator, no matter what the PCs do. The same holds true for the bone troopers, though the skeletal soldiers are too low in rank to know any of the above information.

However, Captain Vesh is carrying a secure computer data module that contains the information the PCs seek. To access it, the data module must first be added to a computer of at least tier 3, requiring a successful DC 25 Computers check to disable or manipulate a module. If the PCs don't have their own tier 3 or higher computer, they'll need to purchase one or arrange to use one. Adding the data module to a lower-tier computer has no effect—the computer is unable to access the data stored on the module.

The data module is equipped with its own countermeasures, including a firewall and a wipe countermeasure. Once properly installed, the data module can be accessed with a successful DC 27 Computers check to hack the system (this assumes the module is installed in a tier 3 computer; if it is installed in a higher-tier computer, you'll need to adjust the DCs to hack the module accordingly). If the PCs fail two attempts to hack the module's firewall, the wipe countermeasure activates, destroying all the data on the module. At this point, the PCs have one last chance to recover the wiped data with a successful DC 37 Computers check.

If the PCs successfully hack Captain Vesh's secure data module, they discover that it contains the data that was deleted from the datacore in the Star-Eater's Spine. This data reveals that the Cult of the Devourer left its Diaspora base to search for the Gate of Twelve Suns in a distant star system called Nejeor, based on the cultists' interpretations of Nyara's prophecies. Nejeor's coordinates put the system somewhere in the Vast. The electronic signature on this data matches that of the hacker who scrubbed the files from the cult's computer system, confirming that the Corpse Fleet visited the Star-Eater's Spine, accessed the datacore, and learned that the cult is searching the Nejeor system for the "key" to the alien superweapon.

If the PCs don't have the hacking skills necessary to crack the secure data module, they can take the module back to Orphys, where Waneda Trux can help them arrange the services of a properly skilled hacker who can provide the PCs with the information they need.

Story Award: For learning the coordinates of the Nejeor system and that the system is the destination of the Corpse Fleet and the Cult of the Devourer, award the PCs 3,200 XP.

CONCLUDING THE ADVENTURE

Once the PCs have defeated Captain Zeera Vesh and her bone troopers, they can return to Orphys with no further difficulties. Allow the PCs to finish any outstanding business they have in the necropolis, but they should remember that both the Cult of the Devourer and the Corpse Fleet have a head start on them. If the PCs don't take the initiative on their own, Chiskisk contacts them in 1d4 days for an update on their mission and to encourage the PCs to pursue their rivals to Nejeor as soon as they are able. Time is of the essence, the shirren again reminds them, and the fact that the Corpse Fleet and the Cult of the Devourer are both one step closer toward finding a worlds-destroying superweapon is not a comforting thought.

If the PCs try to learn more about Nejeor, they can find no information about the system, either on their ship's computer or in Eox's infosphere (or any other Pact World's infosphere, for that matter). It appears that Nejeor is an unexplored system, so to find out more, the PCs will have travel there in person.

Even with the defeat of their primary agent on Eox, the Corpse Fleet has endeavored to prepare for any eventuality—including the fact that Captain Vesh might fail and that the PCs will continue to interfere in their plans. As a result, Corpse Fleet agents surreptitiously placed a tracking device on the PCs' ship during their time on Eox. The device is currently inactive, and there should be no way for the PCs to detect its presence on their ship at this point. But the Corpse Fleet knows the tracking device is there, and it will make use of it later in the campaign to achieve its goals at the expense of the PCs.

For now, the urgency of the PCs' mission to chase the Corpse Fleet and the Cult of the Devourer cannot be underplayed. The quest to find the Gate of Twelve Suns and the Stellar Degenerator will take the heroes to the ruins of an alien city on a distant world in the next volume of the Dead Suns Adventure Path, "The Ruined Clouds."

Treasure: Regardless of whether Chiskisk needs to push the PCs toward Nejeor, the shirren contacts the PCs soon after they finish their mission on Eox to inform the PCs that they have transferred a reward of 2,500 credits apiece to each of the PCs' accounts for their efforts in tracking down the Corpse Fleet and ending the activities of at least one of its agents on Eox.

EOX

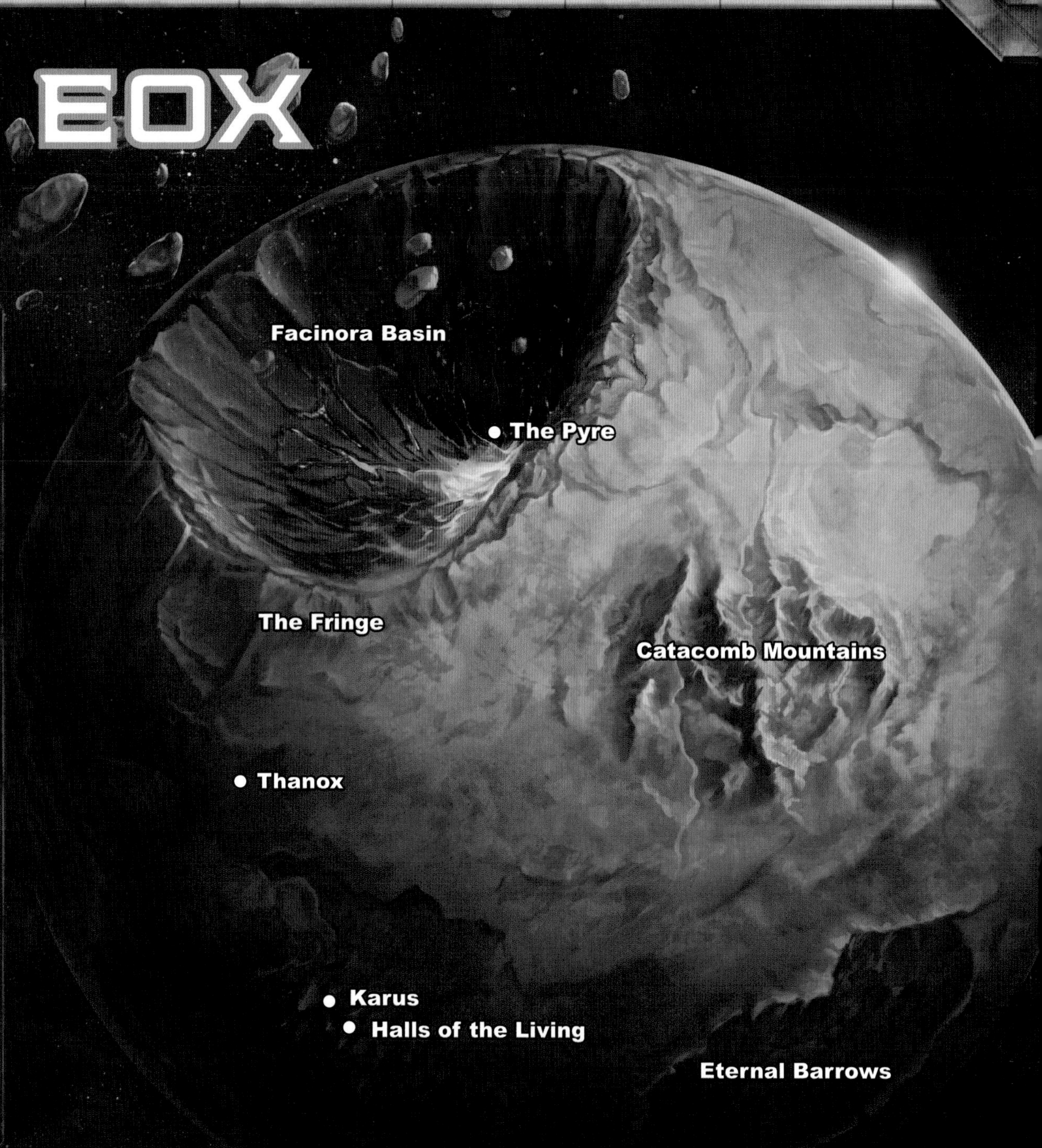

EOX IS AMONG THE MOST MYSTERIOUS OF THE PACT WORLDS, AND IT IS LIKELY THE MEMBER PLANET MOST FEARED BY CITIZENS OF THE REST OF THE SYSTEM. IT IS A DEAD WORLD, KILLED LONG BEFORE THE GAP IN WHAT IS BELIEVED TO HAVE BEEN FALLOUT FROM AN INTERPLANETARY WAR FOUGHT WHEN MOST OF THE PACT WORLDS' IDEA OF ADVANCED TECHNOLOGY WAS LIMITED TO METALLURGY AND PRINTING PRESSES. MOST OF EOX'S INHABITANTS ARE UNDEAD, WITH THE MOST POWERFUL—THE

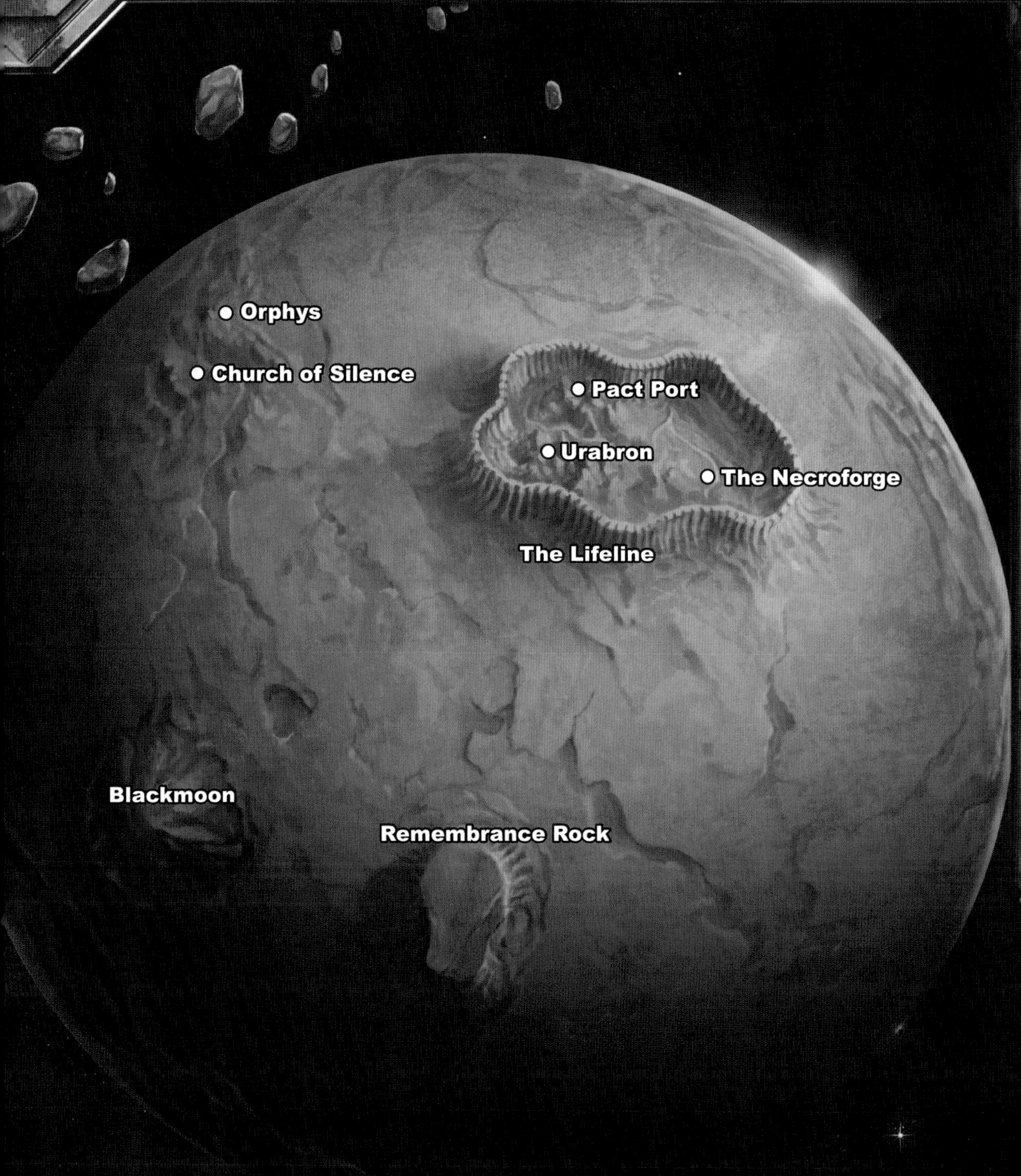

BONE SAGES—SERVING AS REGIONAL LORDS WITH NEAR-ABSOLUTE LOCAL AUTHORITY, THESE CENTURIES-OLD MASTERS OF MAGIC AND TECHNOLOGY BROOK NO INTERFERENCE WITH THEIR PLANS. THEY CAREFULLY KEEP THEIR EXPERIMENTS AND LONG-TERM SCHEMES WITHIN THE BOUNDS OF WHAT THE ABSALOM PACT PERMITS MEMBER WORLDS TO PERFORM IN THEIR OWN TERRITORIES... AND NO OUTSIDERS HAVE SUCCESSFULLY PROVEN OTHERWISE.

More than once in recent centuries, champions of light and virtue have suggested that Eox and its undead populace represent a clear and present danger to all life within the Pact Worlds system. After all, many undead feed on the living, and Eox is one of the few worlds in the system known to have launched planetary assaults against its neighbors, albeit in the past. The idea of accepting a world of undead tyrants as allies does not sit well with many Pact World citizens.

But as the bone sages are fond of reminding other planetary governments, Eox was the very first world to sign the Absalom Pact, and though many Pact World citizens are suspicious of the long-term plans of the denizens of Eox, there is no doubt that their power was instrumental in defending the system, first during conflicts with the Veskarium and later against the first attacks of the Swarm. The bone sages and their animated corpse minions are distasteful to many within the Pact Worlds, but they are careful to maintain diplomatic ties through the system.

Of course, not all members of the Pact Worlds avoid dealing with the undead of Eox. Numerous groups work with citizens of Eox to seek out and oppose the Corpse Fleet, the undead space armada created by defecting soldiers when the bone sages signed the Absalom Pact. Mercenaries and merchants alike appreciate the opportunities provided by the cadaver markets where bodies are bought and sold, the trade in necrograft augmentations and dread technologies shunned on other worlds, and the academies that draw in engineers and spellcasters with their vast stores of knowledge. The few cities on the world—strange sprawling mixes of ancient tombs, high-tech mausoleums, and lifeless offices and factories known collectively as the Necropoleis—are seen as high-risk, high-reward opportunities for the more daring corporations and traders of other Pact Worlds.

The following sections present Eox's two hemispheres, with notable locations and a settlement stat block for the largest and most significant city on the world.

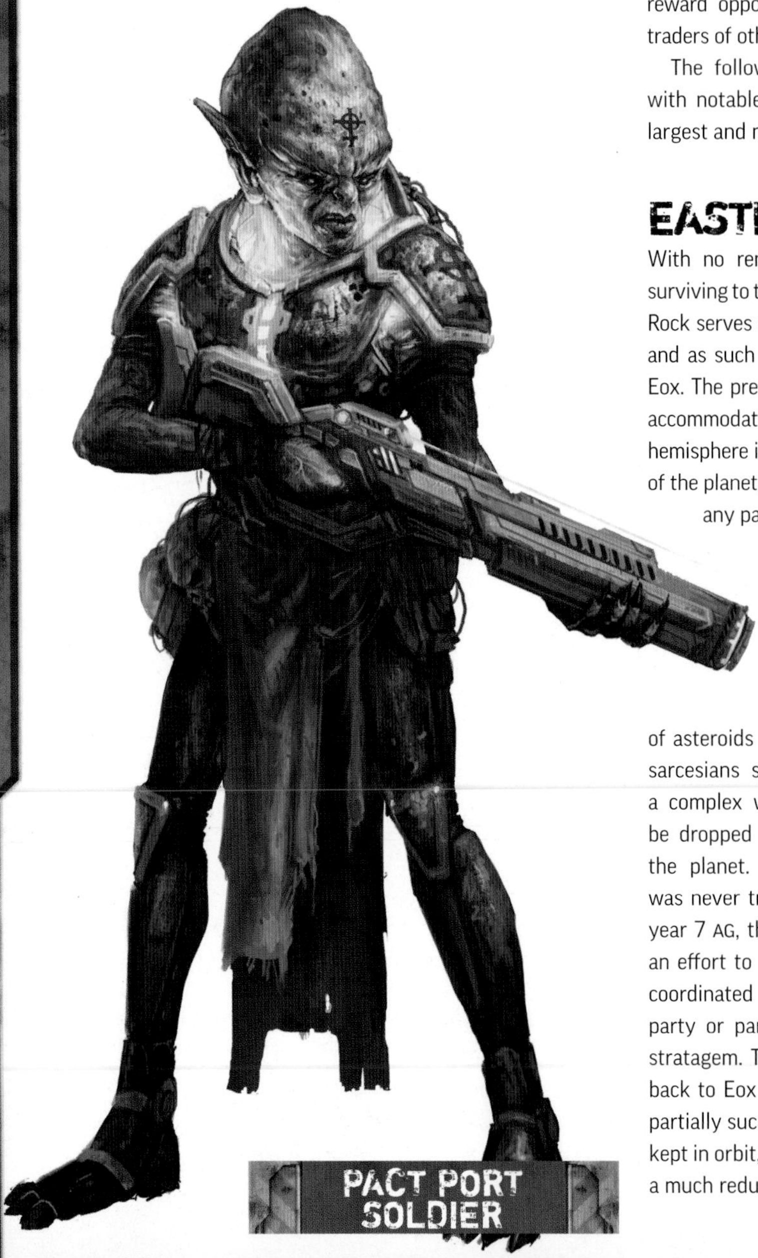

PACT PORT SOLDIER

EASTERN HEMISPHERE

With no remaining seas and little of the planet's history surviving to the modern era, the massive mesa of Remembrance Rock serves as a planetary monument of all that Eox has lost, and as such it is a centerpiece of the eastern hemisphere of Eox. The presence of those few areas on Eox that have some accommodations for living visitors means that the eastern hemisphere is generally considered the safer of the two halves of the planet, though this should not be taken as evidence that any part of Eox is truly safe.

NOTABLE LOCATIONS

The Eastern Hemisphere boasts the following notable locations.

Blackmoon: The cataclysm that killed Eox also created the Thousand Moons, a ring of asteroids around the planet. In the years before the Gap, sarcesians scheming to destroy the bone sages prepared a complex web of magic energies to allow the moons to be dropped on every major necropolis and outpost across the planet. For whatever reason, that planet-killing trap was never triggered—until a few years after the Gap. In the year 7 AG, the bone sages launched the Magefire Assault in an effort to take control of Absalom Station. No nation was coordinated enough to mount an effective defense, but some party or parties unknown managed to set off the ancient stratagem. The bone sages abandoned their attack and fled back to Eox to prevent the devastation, but they were only partially successful. While most of the Thousand Moons were kept in orbit, one of the largest orbiting chunks fell (though at a much reduced speed) and crushed the mighty necropolis of

Murthal, along with everything within 1,000 miles of it. The massive chunk of rock that remained was named Blackmoon, and it is now one of the tallest mountains in the Pact Worlds.

Blackmoon is a nearly hemispherical orb of rock riddled with caves and tunnels that date back to precataclysm Eox. Beneath the stone, some small sections of Murthal survive, cut off from the outside. Rumors suggest there are sarcesian renegades within Blackmoon even now, keeping a watchful eye on the bone sages and preparing for the day the undead betray the Absalom Pact.

Church of Silence: The Church of Silence is an ancient monument to the perfection of undeath, and it has stood for eons as neutral ground among the bone sages as the closest thing to a sacred place the undead of Eox have. It is overseen by the Conclave of Whispers, a respected collection of the oldest bone sages who claim to have given up secular matters in favor of pure research into undeath. The Conclave of Whispers specifically does not include any members of the Eternal Convocation, ensuring that the two groups each work to their own ends, rather than conspiring together. Within the Wordless Halls, the oldest parts of the Church of Silence, the conclave seeks to understand secrets nearly lost to time and to gather all lore on death and undeath available from anywhere in the galaxy. While the Wordless Halls are off limits to most living creatures, the bone sages grant open access to any android, undead, or self-willed robot who wishes to peruse the ancient libraries within and swears to obey the rules of the halls. The outer sections of the Church of Silence have much less lore and material within them, but the bone sages allow living necromancers to petition for access to research specific topics, especially if the practitioners bring some previously unknown bit of undead lore with them to barter for access.

The Lifeline: The Lifeline is a literal line demarcating the safe zone containing the Necroforge, Pact Port, and Urabron. A massive wall—more than 200 feet tall, 50 feet thick, and topped with spiked ridges and defensive plasma turrets—denotes the location of the Lifeline, but these are only the physical portion of the barrier. A magic shield created by dozens of bone sages working in concert exists in the same location, independent of the wall. It prevents the radiation clouds, wild zones of magic, and fields of necromantic energy that plague the rest of Eox from entering the safe zone. The wall is constantly monitored by skeletal guards and ghoul overseers who answer to the Eternal Convocation; they keep out the numerous undead (and few living) threats that run wild in the lawless places of Eox. The atmosphere within the safe zone is still thin and poisonous, but the Lifeline keeps many of the dangers of Eox at bay, allowing visitors to move more freely and safely between the region's three settlements.

The Necroforge: The Necroforge is less a city than it is an extensive industrial complex dedicated to the creation and study of undead, necrografts, and necromantic magic. Along with Orphys, it is one of the primary destinations for living beings who wish to augment themselves with necromantic implants and necromancers who seek to become undead (often at the price of a century of unliving service once their transformation is complete), as well as body merchants who bring corpses to Eox to be turned into new undead citizens into components for necrografts and other experiments. Though very few living creatures permanently dwell in the Necroforge, it has extensive facilities to house and entertain its clients, guests, trade partners, and visitors. The Necroforge is ruled by the Painted Lady, a bone sage who maintains a nearly living appearance and has adorned her entire body with dozens of gruesome tattoos.

Orphys: Orphys is the largest and most prosperous of Eox's few cities and is home to the Eternal Convocation, the council of bone sages who assign Eoxian ambassadors to other Pact Worlds and appoint representatives to the Pact Council on Absalom Station. The Eternal Convocation also rules Orphys directly, making it the only major necropolis not controlled by a single bone sage.

All of Orphys is enclosed within a bubble of breathable atmosphere, making it one of the most common destinations for living visitors outside of the Lifeline. Given that Orphys is as close to a planetary capital as Eox offers, most citizens of the Pact Worlds believe the necrovites who rule the city maintain the atmosphere to encourage living tourism and make it easier for Pact World officials to interface with their Eoxian counterparts. In truth, the Eternal Convocation doesn't much care how the atmosphere impacts the daily lives of living visitors. The bubble was established centuries ago as part of an experiment into how various conditions impact the long-term stability and potential decay of undead bodies, and that experiment has continued uninterrupted for hundreds of years.

Unlike for cities within the Lifeline, Orphys's infrastructure does little to accommodate living residents beyond providing a suitable atmosphere. Food vendors are rare and deal almost exclusively in preserved foods. Even so, it is far easier to maintain livable conditions here than in nearly any other necropolis, and Orphys has built a number of businesses around the potential opportunities living creatures present. It and the Necroforge are the two major hubs in the necrograft trade, and Orphys contains administrative and business centers that allow Pact World companies and organizations to interact with the Eternal Convocation.

Pact Port: Pact Port is the lone city on Eox that is not part of the Necropoleis. It is designed primarily as a landing place for Pact Worlds trade ships and for the warehousing of Eoxian goods for export. Pact Port is a small domed city of 100,000 denizens, more than half living, and is administered by the ghoul Sadrat Phain in the name of the Conclave of Whispers. Within the dome, air designed to support as many forms of life native to the Pact Worlds as possible is maintained. Sadrat is permissive about most issues; other than those laws required by the Absalom Pact, the only law enforced is a strict ban on removing relics of ancient Eox from the world without the approval of the Convocation.

Remembrance Rock: An enormous mesa created by the energies of the cataclysm, Remembrance Rock is a massive raised mesa riddled with monuments and tombs to all that was lost when Eox was killed. Most of the tombs and shrines have long stood empty, but a few deep in the interior are still protected by active guardians.

Urabron: Urabron is a small settlement that predates the construction of the Lifeline. It is ruled by the bone sage Quatherat Hafet, an undead who is more machine than corpse. Hafet claims to have existed for eons before the Gap, and he shrugs off questions about the missing centuries of his memory. Urabron is small enough that it can be encased by a single large dome that maintains heat and an atmosphere similar to that of Castrovel, and it houses a few thousand scholars and spellcasters who study with the bone troopers who serve Hafet. Why he allows such study or lets Urabron be included within the area of the Lifeline is unknown.

THE PYRE

ORPHYS

NE necropolis

Population 1,450,000 (88% undead, 7% android, 5% other)

Government oligarchy

Qualities academic, polluted, technologically advanced

Maximum Item Level 18th

WESTERN HEMISPHERE

The western hemisphere of Eox is hotter and more toxic than the eastern hemisphere, in large part due to the still-seething lava sea of the Facinora Basin but also due to lava vents, which are more common between the Fringe mountain range and the Eternal Barrows than anywhere else on the planet. Clouds of poisonous and radioactive gases are also common throughout this hemisphere, making travel very dangerous for the living.

NOTABLE LOCATIONS

The following sites of the Western Hemisphere are the most interesting amid the blasted landscape.

Catacomb Mountains: It is well documented that the Catacomb Mountains did not exist prior to the Gap. The lands where these imposing and angular slabs of basalt and black quartz now rise up were once a barren plain of radioactive lowlands and poisonous clouds. No record exists of why or how they were constructed—but they are certainly not natural. The Catacomb Mountains are a manufactured range of rock and strange ores honeycombed with hundreds of thousands of tombs, most sealed with advanced security systems and magic glyphs. Early expeditions into the outermost tombs revealed them to be filled with the remains of destroyed undead, often sealed in computerized sarcophagi designed to douse the corpses with acid or flame at any sign of movement. Other tombs were empty, with Eoxian runes warning that "necrovores have escaped" and similar vague messages. A joint agreement made by the most powerful bone sages forbids any further exploration, but it is strongly suspected that numerous secret expeditions are undertaken every year.

Eternal Barrows: When Eox joined the Pact Worlds, not all bone sages agreed with the decision. Though the Eternal Convocation and Conclave of Whispers both supported the idea, many bone sages felt it placed them in a position of weakness. The details of the brief, vicious conflict that followed have been kept from the living, but it is known that multitudes of undead on the losing side were imprisoned in the massive field of penal tombs known as the Eternal Barrows. The most powerful undead prisoners, including ghosts, necrovites, nightshades, and vampires, were placed in stasis tombs so they would not experience the passage of time. The bone sages surrounded upstart undead masters with vast vaults; each of these vaults contained lesser undead creatures that did not answer to the undead master contained within, thus avoiding the possibility of collusion.

The ruling bone sages of Eox ensure that the deepest of the Eternal Barrows are untouched, and they seem unconcerned with how many centuries might pass before the undead who opposed them could be released. Many admit that destroying their political opponents would not be worth losing the vast knowledge those undead hold, and some even hint that the most powerful of those imprisoned can't be destroyed by any force. But with no fear of the ravages of time, the rulers of Eox are content to allow their foes to be locked away until the situation changes, maybe centuries or eons from now.

Halls of the Living: The Halls of the Living are an aberration on Eox—a subterranean city designed and maintained purely for the benefit of its living inhabitants. However, it is not exactly a city where most people would choose to live, as it is maintained only as a backdrop for the cruel games and invasive reality shows that are the primary entertainment on Eox and are broadcast throughout the Pact Worlds. Many of the transmissions are outlawed on other planets, but little can be done to prevent them from being sent, and even the most depraved recordings can easily be found in archives of illicit sections of the infospheres of most Pact World cities.

Though numerous groups protest the existence of the Halls of the Living, as an entirely local issue, they are not a violation of the Absalom Pact. Further, every citizen is—at least officially—a willing participant. Children born within the Halls of the Living are removed to state-funded quarters in Urabron and not allowed to return until they reach the age of maturity. Anyone else is free to go at any time and receives a complementary one-way ticket to Absalom Station... and little else. Despite this, the potential fame and fortune that participants can earn in just a few years of games and programs has fostered a long list of petitioners waiting to join the halls. Those citizens who manage to build a fanbase of viewers and patrons can often skip the deadlier shows and instead participate in live feeds of their day-to-day activities or skill-based entertainment contests.

The vast majority of participants are humans and vesk (who seem to relish the challenges), but a noteworthy number of dwarves, Forlorn elves, lashuntas, and ysoki also participate. Undead are forbidden (though undead camera crews, guards, showrunners, and administrators operate within the city for specific broadcasts) and androids and kasathas are very rare. A small number of living elebrians—the dominant race of Eox before the disaster that killed the world—also participate and has done so for centuries. However, it is whispered that none of the elebrians in the Halls of the Living are true surviving members of that race and that all those who claim to be are either undead in disguise or surgically altered humans.

Karus: Karus was originally constructed around and on top of the Halls of the Living, and for centuries it existed purely as a place for the undead of Eox to gather to view the events the denizens of the halls undergo for the undead's entertainment. Since it was one of the few places bone sages peacefully gathered, over the centuries it also became a place where they could meet in neutral territory to form councils and make treaties. As a result, Karus was the center from which the Sleepless Watch formed to oversee control of the Sentinel, a moon-sized defense platform that was ancient even before the cataclysm struck Eox centuries prior to the Gap. The settlement expanded well beyond the Halls of the Living, in time growing to be an entirely separate complex.

When Eox signed the Absalom Pact, one of the most powerful dissenting bone sages was the Festrog Queen, who felt that agreeing to a treaty with any living creature was an affront to her undead perfection. Rather than confront her and attempt to banish her to the Eternal Barrows, the newly formed Eternal Convocation offered to salve her dignity by granting her control of Karus, and thus the greatest say in the control of the Sentinel. Whether the Festrog Queen saw opposition to the Convocation as doomed to failure or she was truly mollified, she accepted the tribute and has ruled Karus for over 250 years. Both because of her true dislike of the living and as a security measure, the Festrog Queen has outlawed the living within Karus, restricting them to the nearby Halls of the Living.

The Pyre: The Pyre is the only settlement within the Facinora Basin, a vast sea of lava that dates back to the cataclysm. A massive tower stretching more than a mile up from the lava, the Pyre is an arcology—a self-sufficient building that houses an entire city. It is one of the primary sources of power on Eox, using the heat of the endlessly churning lava to incinerate waste materials from all over the planet (according to legend, including the bodies of any undead the bone sages do not wish to see again) to form a massive tornado of flame that drives hundreds of turbines before being vented into the Eoxian sky as an eternal pillar of fire. The Pyre is ruled by Kalantrodoch the Unburning, a necrovite less than a century old who focuses almost exclusively on technological advancements rather than magical ones. Kalantrodoch rarely allows visitors or tourists within the Pyre's walls, except for those who pique his well-known curiosity regarding pre-Gap technology.

Thanox: One of dozens of midsize necropolises scattered across Eox, Thanox is ruled by the bone sage referred to only as the Soulless One. In the minutes after the Gap, the Soulless One moved with decisive force and claimed the city from its former ruler. Such conflicts between bone sages are unremarkable, but the Soulless One was the first undead to claim the rank of bone sage without being some form of lich or necrovite. Instead, he is a shadowy apparition with bright-green circuitry patterns forming his eyes and running along his shoulders and arms. The Soulless One successfully played his foes off one another in political maneuvers until his strong support of the Eox's signing of the Absalom Pact cemented his place among the ruling class.

NECROGRAFTS

Necrografts are augmentations utilizing undead organs and necromantic rituals rather than technology. They were invented on Eox, and they are most commonly available in Orphys and at the Necroforge within the Lifeline on Eox. Most Pact Worlds outlaw the creation and installation of necrografts (though not their possession), but they can still be found in some less reputable back-alley augmentation clinics.

Necrografts follow the existing rules for augmentations (see page 208 of the *Starfinder Core Rulebook*), but they use different components than biotech and cybernetics. Any biotech or cybernetic augmentation can be created as a necrograft and installed for only 90% of the augmentation's normal cost, but doing so causes the recipient to gain the necrograft subtype (see below). Necrografts have the same system limitations all augmentations share.

For those low on funds, some bone sages and corporations on Eox are willing to defer the cost of travel to Eox and augmentation for any client who signs a corpse-lease agreement. Necrograft versions of standard prosthetic limbs (see page 210 of the *Starfinder Core Rulebook*), and necrograft ears, eyes, or tongues (which use the same mechanics as prosthetic limbs but serve as sensory organs) can even be implanted with no up-front cost. However, the corpse-lease agreement states that if the recipient dies before paying off all the costs associated with the travel and augmentation, the leasing Eoxian group owns the patient's body, which it then uses in creating undead servitors or more necrografts. More advanced necrografts aren't generally available without payment in full (though complementary travel is likely to still be offered to customers within the Pact Worlds).

NECROGRAFT SUBTYPE

Adding even a single necrograft to a living body causes the recipient creature to gain the necrograft subtype. Abilities, items, and spells that detect or identify undead reveal necrografts (identifying only the augmentations as undead, rather than the recipient creature as a whole).

Creatures with this subtype are also damaged by spells that damage undead, and can be subjected to other undead-specific effects. If a spell or ability that does something other than deal damage would not normally affect such a creature, but does affect undead, the creature can be targeted, but it gains a bonus to its AC and saving throw against the effect equal to 4 – the number of necrografts it has (to a minimum bonus of +0).

NECROGRAFT-ONLY AUGMENTATIONS

In addition to necrograft versions of typical biotech and cybernetics, there are many unique necrografts that can be created only using necromancy. These necrografts all come in five possible models (mk 1 through mk 5) and vary in price by model as detailed below.

MODEL	LEVEL	PRICE
Mk 1	1	200
Mk 2	6	4,000
Mk 3	12	30,000
Mk 4	18	350,000
Mk 5	20	775,000

NECROGRAFT DESCRIPTIONS

The augmentations detailed below are available only as necrografts. If a necrograft's effect requires a saving throw, the save DC equals 10 + half the necrograft's item level + the recipient's key ability score modifier.

BLACK HEART

SYSTEM Heart or Lungs

Despite its name, a black heart can augment any major circulatory organ that helps sustain life in a living creature, though it most commonly augments a heart. A black heart is a strip of necromancy-infused undead flesh that turns whatever organ it is attached to a deep shade of ebony.

A creature with a black heart gains the benefits of the environmental protections of armor (see page 196 of the *Starfinder Core Rulebook*), which last for a number of days equal to double the necrograft's item level. A black heart automatically recharges 1 hour of this duration for each hour this ability is not in use (up to its normal maximum). Additionally, the recipient gains an enhancement bonus to saving throws against death effects, disease, mind-affecting effects, paralysis, poison, sleep effects, and stunning effects equal to the necrograft's mark, unless the effect specifies it functions against undead.

BONE BLADE

SYSTEM Arm

	DAMAGE		
MODEL	STANDARD	HEAVY	CRITICAL
Mk 1	1d4 S	2d4 S	Staggered
Mk 2	1d8 S	2d8 S	Staggered
Mk 3	2d8 S	4d8 S	Stunned
Mk 4	5d8 S	7d8 S	Stunned
Mk 5	5d10 S	7d10 S	Stunned

Bone blades are weapons built into undead arms that are then grafted onto their recipients. The blade can be retracted into the limb (making it impossible to notice without a careful inspection, scan, spell, or similar ability) or extended from the wrist for combat. Extending or retracting a bone blade is a swift action, and the recipient can't use the hand of the associated arm to hold anything or perform fine manipulation when the blade is extended. A bone blade cannot be disarmed, but it can be sundered. When a bone blade's recipient regains Hit Points (whether through first aid, magic, or natural healing), the blade regains the same number of Hit Points. If destroyed, the bone blade regrows in 24 hours.

Standard bone blades are one-handed simple melee weapons with the operative weapon special property. It is possible to have a more complex heavy bone blade installed, which changes the bone blade into a one-handed advanced melee weapon. These heavy bone blades are not operative weapons, but they deal more damage (see the table above). There is no difference in cost between standard and heavy bone blades, but the decision between them must be made when the bone blade is installed and cannot be changed.

GHOUL GLANDS

SYSTEM
Skin

Ghoul glands are a series of hundreds of tiny undead sweat glands, which are installed all over the recipient's skin. The glands pull energy from the body and mind of the recipient and use it to create a staggering or paralyzing effect. As a standard action a number of times per day equal to the necrograft's mark, the recipient can activate the glands and attempt to touch a foe (doing so requires a successful attack roll against the target's KAC). The target must succeed at a Fortitude saving throw or be staggered (for mk 1 through mk 3 ghoul glands) or stunned (for mk 4 and mk 5 ghoul glands) for 1d4 rounds.

GRAVE WIND

SYSTEM
Lungs

MODEL	DISEASE
Mk 1	Filth fever
Mk 2	Cackle fever
Mk 3	Devil chills
Mk 4	Demon fever
Mk 5	Mummy rot

A grave wind necrograft replaces the recipient's lungs with black, undead lungs that can still pump air and oxygenate blood but are also able to exhale a diseased miasma. As a standard action a number of times per day equal to the necrograft's mark, the recipient can expose an adjacent creature to a necromantic disease. The disease inflicted depends on the model of the grave wind, as indicated in the table above.

These necromantic diseases act as the normal diseases of the same name (see page 418 of the *Starfinder Core Rulebook*), except for the following. The save DC is determined by the necrograft and its recipient. No wound or actual transfer of air is necessary for the disease to affect a target; even someone in armor with its environmental seals active can be exposed. A creature infected with such a disease is not a carrier, so it can't pass the disease on to other victims. Creatures immune to death effects are immune to these diseases, and any bonus a creature has to saving throws against death effects applies to saves against these diseases (however, the diseases don't count as death effects for other purposes, such as *raise dead*).

SHADOW NERVES

SYSTEM
Spinal Column

Shadow nerves are long strands of partially incorporeal undead nerve fibers that have strong connections to the Shadow Plane. Shadow nerves allow the recipient to navigate a path that exists partially in the Material Plane and partially in the Shadow Plane. A number of times per day equal to the necrograft's mark, the recipient can take a guarded step of 10 feet, rather than the normal 5-foot guarded step (see page 247 of the *Starfinder Core Rulebook*), as long as the recipient is not in an area of bright light.

VAMPIRE VOICE

SYSTEM
Throat

A vampire voice necrograft attaches to the recipient's vocal cords, granting a supernaturally threatening tone. While most recipients of vampire voices are convinced their necrografts came from vampire spawn, creators of these undead augmentations never promise any such lofty origins.

A vampire voice grants an enhancement bonus to Intimidate checks equal to the necrograft's mark. The recipient of a vampire voice can also use Intimidate to bully a foe without sharing a language. If the attempt is successful, a single simple request can be conveyed along with the bullying (such as "go away" or "don't hurt him"), though specific or complex requests can't be made without sharing a language. Once a creature has been the target of a bullying attempt by a recipient with a vampire voice, it can't be targeted by this ability from the same recipient again for 24 hours.

WRAITH MOTES

SYSTEM
Eyes

Wraith motes replace the recipient's eyes with glowing red motes of fiery-red light, which smolder and produce thin trails of white smoke. Wraith motes allow the recipient to retain all her natural vision abilities, but they can also augment her vision for a number of minutes per day equal to the necrograft's mark. They can be activated as a swift action, or they can be activated as a reaction whenever the recipient attempts a Perception check. They can be deactivated as a swift action. The wraith motes' duration need not be used all at once, but it must be used in 1-minute increments.

The vision granted by the wraith motes varies based on the model as follows. Higher-level models can be used to grant the vision options of lower-level version, but only a single benefit can be gained at a time. Mk 1 wraith motes grant low-light vision. Mk 2 wraith motes grant darkvision with a range of 60 feet. Mk 3 wraith motes grant the see in darkness universal creature ability (allowing the recipient to see perfectly in darkness of any kind, including magical darkness; see page 156 of the *Starfinder Alien Archive*). Mk 4 wraith motes grant the ability to see invisible creatures and objects (as per *see invisibility*). Mk 5 wraith motes allow the recipient to see into both the Ethereal Plane and Shadow Plane.

THE CORPSE FLEET

The aptly named Corpse Fleet is composed of renegade undead who broke off from Eox's navy when their home planet signed the Absalom Pact. Refusing to cooperate with the inferior worlds of the living, the first defectors disappeared beyond the edges of the solar system. In the depths of space, the newly formed Corpse Fleet regrouped and swore to oppose the unity of the Pact Worlds and their former foes in the Veskarium, as well as all other living threats. Many members of the Corpse Fleet, except for those undead recently animated as part of the fleet's ongoing operations, view themselves as exiled from the almost spiritually sacred soil of Eox.

HISTORY

The historic Absalom Pact was signed 5 years following the Battle of Aledra, the first major confrontation between the forces of the Golarion System and the Veskarium. Not all inhabitants of the signatory worlds were content with the agreement, especially senior military commanders of Eox's ever-expanding navy. Unlike the fleets of many of the Golarion System's other worlds, the Eoxian Navy had held its own against the hostile Veskarium. To see their victories sullied by the "mewling infants" of other worlds chafed many Eoxian admirals and commodores, resulting in their sudden defection.

How the Corpse Fleet managed to mobilize and escape the attention of the nascent Stewards is a mystery lost amid the chaos of the signing of the Absalom Pact. Less trusting members of the Pact Worlds posit that the Corpse Fleet was unofficially sanctioned by several of the ruling bone sages of Eox, specifically those who remained skeptical of the Pact Worlds' potential to triumph over the vesk. This theory suggests that the Corpse Fleet was given sufficient material and political backing to depart the system and travel into deep space, where it would await the results of further hostilities between the Pact Worlds and the Veskarium.

If the Pact's efforts failed, then the Eoxians could still call in a sizable reserve of ships to defend their world—all without risking their full assets in the defense of other planets.

The bone sages maintain to this very day that the legal leadership of Eox never endorsed the Corpse Fleet. The first sightings of the undead armada following the Absalom Pact's signing were during the tumultuous time of the Stardust Plague. Heavily modified ships, clearly Eoxian in origin, raided dozens of plague-ridden carriers and bulk transports. The Stewards investigated what few coherent reports of Corpse Fleet sightings they received, but they could never pin down the renegade undead navy in an engagement. Meanwhile, the Corpse Fleet harvested thousands of ill people, offering them the salvation of undeath in exchange for service. Over 2 decades, the Corpse Fleet's numbers swelled due to the sickened living seeking salvation from death.

In the following centuries, travelers discovered Corpse Fleet facilities across Near Space and the Vast. These explorers, particularly members of the Starfinder Society, often reported finding abandoned structures of Eoxian design on planets previously uncharted by the Pact Worlds. All traces of useful information regarding the Corpse Fleet had already been stripped from these discovered structures, the fleet having long since moved on. The infamous Starfinder Historia-4 compiled a large dataset for the *Starfinder Chronicles* detailing the change from standard Eoxian construction methods based on dating the structures—the older the structure, the more it adhered to known Eoxian standards, while newer structures diverged into previously unseen designs.

Whether suspicions surrounding the Corpse Fleet's true loyalty to the Eoxian bone sages were correct is now irrelevant. The appearance of the Swarm provided the last chance for the renegade fleet to return to the Pact Worlds in defense of their former home world. Instead, the Corpse Fleet remains at a well-measured distance from the advancing Swarm, content to continue their efforts in raiding forces of the Pact Worlds and the Veskarium. Exactly what involvement the Corpse Fleet will have in the ongoing war against the Swarm remains—like most of the Corpse Fleet's actions—a mystery.

STRUCTURE AND RANKS

When the first admirals and captains departed the Eoxian Navy to form the Corpse Fleet, they brought their military order and ranks with them. In the intervening centuries, the structure of the Corpse Fleet stabilized, with a distinct military hierarchy that imitates the navy from which it derived. At the head of this organization is the Undying Admiral, the overseer of all Corpse Fleet operations. While ostensibly advised by various supporting admirals, the Undying Admiral is solely responsible for coordinating the individual task forces of the Corpse Fleet.

Supporting the Undying Admiral and his orders are the various admirals of the Corpse Fleet. Each admiral is responsible for a task force of several dozen Corpse Fleet starships. The admirals maintain relative autonomy with their assigned task forces, each directing their respective armadas to accomplish objectives set forth by the Undying Admiral. To ensure the continued survival of the Corpse Fleet, admirals rarely work in the same system as one another, and task-force fleets act independently to prevent enemy forces from pinning the entirety of the Corpse Fleet in a single engagement. Some outsiders mistakenly assume this means the Corpse Fleet operates in small groups; the truth is that even a single task force is as large as entire defense fleets of Pact World organizations.

Rear admirals and commodores command fleets of four to eight starships. These detached armadas are sent on long-term missions away from their originating task force. The rank of rear admiral is awarded to members of the Corpse Fleet assigned to extended sojourns from the parent task force. These small fleets operate beyond the scope of their fellow undead for decades at a time. Conversely, commodores have direct command over similarly sized portions of a task force, though these fleets rarely see deployments longer than 1 to 2 months. Otherwise, when acting within the task force, commodores manage the orders assigned to their ships during fleet engagements.

It falls to captains to command the individual ships of the Corpse Fleet. Assisting each captain is a commander, who focuses on motivating the ship's crew, either through fear or by fostering intense loyalty. Admirals create captain-and-commander pairings of differing dispositions, as the balance often ensures a suitable mix of caution and ferocity in combat situations. Below the rank of commander are the lieutenant commanders who manage distinct operations. On Corpse Fleet battleships, lieutenant commanders typically hold each non-captain starship role (engineer, gunner, pilot, and science officer), commanding shifts of grunts who perform the many complicated tasks involved in maintaining and operating large vessels.

Lieutenants and ensigns are the lowest ranks in the Corpse Fleet. Ensigns perform a number of roles, acting as reserves and students under superior officers. Lieutenants fill key positions within the naval assets of the Corpse Fleet but also act as ground-based specialists. Most officers of the Corpse Fleet operating outside of a starship are either lieutenants or converted—the enlisted branch of the Corpse Fleet. Mystics of Urgathoa, trained assassin operatives, and soldiers replete with necrotech arms and armor are the most common of the Corpse Fleet's ground agents. Some lieutenants choose never to serve aboard a starship, instead focusing their efforts on surface operations. These officers are very rarely awarded with promotions to the rank of commander, and only a select few ever ascend to the rank of captain.

The converted are the mindless or near-mindless undead created by the Corpse Fleet's brutal necromantic tactics. When a boarding action is deemed necessary by a Corpse Fleet captain, hordes of skeletons and zombies flood enemy starships. These boarders engage in horrific hand-to-hand combat, often supported by scores of ghoul ensigns bearing necrotech firearms. Sometimes, this carnage is enough to corrupt the slaughtered souls into undead, but usually this conversion requires high-level mystics to cast *animate dead* on the fallen. Most vessels don't carry such mystics, so the most viable dead are carried back to a base or capital starship, where such spellcasters are more common.

GOALS

The Undying Admiral sets forth the great endeavors of the Corpse Fleet. Each task force is deployed to oversee a given project. The first great mission was to establish a series of hidden installations and outposts throughout Near Space and the Vast. These secretive locations house the factories and shipyards of the Corpse Fleet, each of which is a necrotech masterpiece that required decades of dedicated construction to complete. For an example of one such location, see the Codex of Worlds on page 61. For every completed munitions factory or shipyard, a dozen abandoned Corpse Fleet structures mire the stars. Such facilities are landmarks of the Corpse Fleet's continued evolution, with each forgotten installation stripped of equipment to forge newer and more efficient production facilities elsewhere.

To this day, the Corpse Fleet seeks to maintain a steady supply of converted troops and starship officers. The fleet might never have reached its current numbers were it not for the bountiful humanoid harvests reaped during the Stardust Plague. In the years since, Corpse Fleet task forces have dispatched commodores to head small fleets sent to harvest living beings from the Pact Worlds and the wider galaxy, as the ongoing conflict between the Corpse Fleet and the Stewards and the Knights of Golarion ensures that the undead require constant replenishment of soldiers to maintain their offensive capabilities.

Beyond the Corpse Fleet's need for production facilities and its morbid means of recruitment, there exists one primary goal for the fleet: to shatter the unity of the Pact Worlds. By ending the Absalom Pact, members of the Corpse Fleet believe they can return their home world, Eox, to its former glory. To achieve this monumental task, the Corpse Fleet strives to construct an armada of such size that it can rival the combined fleets of the Pact Worlds. While such an accomplishment could take centuries of construction and corpse harvesting, some task-force fleets are assigned other missions to speed up the endeavor, operating under the supervision of admirals seeking to uncover hidden magic or technology capable of either destroying the forces of the Pact Worlds or forcing their subservience to Eox.

IMPORTANT MEMBERS

Thousands of undead agents serve as officers or converted members of the Corpse Fleet. Some of the fleet's most important and influential members are described below.

Admiral Morbari Coranith (NE female elebrian ghast mystic): The worship of Urgathoa is one of many links between officers of the Corpse Fleet and the people of Eox. Coranith received the macabre blessing of the Pallid Princess in the earliest stages of her undeath. She directs her task force in an ongoing search for artifacts of religious or spiritual significance, believing they contain power that can give the Corpse Fleet the edge it needs to defeat the Pact Worlds. The ships of her fleet are replete with followers of Urgathoa, each capable of casting powerful spells to wound intruders and repair the unliving. Morbari leads her operations from the *Dark Reliquary*, a unique carrier filled with Necrofighters (see page 50).

Admiral Vurannka (NE female elebrian bone trooper technomancer): While Vurannka never reached the elevated position of bone sage, she was still very influential in Eoxian politics before she left to join the Corpse Fleet. She brought a number of Eoxian vessels and troops with her and was rewarded with the position of admiral despite not being very keen on fighting. From aboard the bridge of the bulk freighter *Soul Glutton*, Vurannka organizes much of the Corpse Fleet's operations, deciding when to build or abandon production facilities and the best locations for these structures, which are the undead navy's metaphorical lifeblood.

Captain Inu-Szar (NE female elebrian bone trooper envoy): The captain of the *Osseous Branch*, a Corpse Fleet cruiser, Inu-Szar is one of the few diplomats in the fleet. Her ship can host living creatures—a rarity among the vessels of the Corpse Fleet. Inu-Szar is a ruthless diplomat, focusing her efforts on extending the reach of the Corpse Fleet into the deepest reaches of the Vast. She specializes in forging temporary alliances with species that have assets or technology valuable to the Corpse Fleet. Her negotiations have seeded agreements and alliances with several races and empires otherwise ambivalent to the Corpse Fleet's undead nature.

Captain Kovlov Amalan (LE male vesk corpsefolk mechanic): A seasoned campaigner within the Veskarium's forces, Kovlov Amalan was infamous for finishing battles despite suffering severe wounds. His luck ran out in the Battle of Aledra as his squad struggled against a tide of Eoxian soldiers. When Amalan rose from death as an intelligent zombie, he was recruited by Eox to fight against his former comrades. Still eager for battle, he agreed and was among those who defected with the signing of the Absalom Pact. Amalan now serves as the captain of the *Last Breath*, a corpse-collection vessel. The *Last Breath* roves the galaxy, scouring the spaceways for forgotten battlegrounds, lost colonies, and wrecked starships to harvest the remains of once-living creatures that would otherwise eventually turn to dust. Such corpses are either reanimated by Corpse Fleet necromancers or serve as grist for the undead navy's own necrograft factories.

Captain Xorketh (CE android vampire soldier): Xorketh was once a member of the Android Abolitionist Front, operating out of the Diaspora. A chance encounter with a Corpse Fleet infiltrator ended their life and ultimately resulted in the android being reanimated as an undead with a thirst for blood. With few options, Xorketh sought out the Corpse Fleet, enlisting as an officer to satiate their new addiction. Putting their knowledge of slaver tactics and countertactics to use, Xorketh quickly became one of the Corpse Fleet's most skilled agents in the art of harvesting new undead for the ranks of the converted. They've since ascended to the rank of captain, commanding the battleship *Mortality's Mill*, a grotesque derivative of an Eoxian Thaumtech Omenbringer chassis (*Core Rulebook* 307) that specializes in vicious boarding and body-harvesting operations across the galaxy.

Lieutenant Ravitious (NE male wraith operative): Almost every form of undead has a place in the Corpse Fleet, though those few incorporeal undead have difficulty assisting in the physical operation of a starship. Ravitious's living identity has been lost to time. He operates under direct orders from the admirals of the Corpse Fleet, routinely redeployed to the command of different officers in need of his specialized skills. Ravitious uses his incorporeal nature to board enemy starships, focusing his attention on disabling engines or shields. Against larger enemy targets, he leads a squad of similarly incorporeal Corpse Fleet agents to ensure the success of his sabotage operations. Rare are the souls who can keep calm in the face of a Corpse Fleet armada—rarer are those who keep calm against a Corpse Fleet armada and an incursion of ghostly saboteurs.

The Perpetual Mass (NE occult zombie oma): Oma (*Starfinder Alien Archive* 88), also known as "space whales," are immense beings that can survive in and travel through the vast inky void of space. The Corpse Fleet had the fortune to come across and defeat one such creature in recent years in a massive naval engagement. Rather than simply leave the oma's corpse to rot, the Corpse Fleet turned its considerable necromantic skill toward reanimating the vast stellar beast. Now known only as the Perpetual Mass, this creature is the zombified remains of an oma, further augmented with plates of bone and steel commonly seen in Eoxian starship design. Half zombie and half starship, this creature now serves as an undead siege vessel and is one of the largest ships in the entirety of the Corpse Fleet.

Undying Admiral Shathrava (LE male elebrian necrovite technomancer): Once a powerful bone sage on Eox, Shathrava oversaw a vast territory prior to the signing of the Absalom Pact. He sought a policy of isolationism in the face of the Veskarium's assault on the Golarion System, which ultimately distanced him from the other bone sages. Recognizing that events would soon force a detente with the inferior living beings of the other worlds of the system, Shathrava forged a coalition of key officers from the Eoxian Navy and departed the system, forming the Corpse Fleet. To this day, he directs Corpse Fleet operations, maintaining regular contact with his allies and servitors on Eox. Returning to his home world is the guiding purpose of Shathrava's actions, though he will do so only when he can assure Eox's dominance over the revolting living members of the Pact Worlds.

UNDYING ADMIRAL SHATHRAVA

MILITARY NECROTECH

The Corpse Fleet employs several necrotech creations in its unending operations, infusing necromantic effects into much of its standard-issue equipment. Presented below are several weapons originally manufactured in Corpse Fleet facilities. These items are generally difficult to find in the Pact Worlds, with the exception of major cities on Eox.

CORPSE FLEET EQUIPMENT

The Corpse Fleet uses a broad array of weapons in their shadow war against the Pact Worlds. Undead officers maintain a fondness for cryo weapons that stems from the innate immunity bone troopers have to cold damage. Several admirals are already equipping their soldiers with a new variant of cryo weapon unique to the factories of the Corpse Fleet: the frailty series. These weapons are constructed using foul Urgathoan rites and blasphemies against Pharasma, imparting their frigid blasts with the chill of death and making undead not just immune to their damage but actually able to gain temporary vitality from their blasts.

Several Corpse Fleet weapons have the necrotic weapon special property.

Necrotic: A necrotic weapon deals cold damage infused with negative energy. Creatures immune to negative energy (such as the targets of a *death ward* spell) are immune to the cold damage of a necrotic weapon, and the cold damage of necrotic weapons affects only living creatures. Undead creatures targeted by a weapon with this property not only take no damage from the cold but also gain temporary Hit Points equal to the weapon's item level. These temporary Hit Points last for 10 minutes, until expended, or until the undead gains a larger number of temporary Hit Points from a necrotic weapon. A creature can benefit from only one source of temporary Hit Points from a necrotic weapon at a time.

DUELING SWORD

The dueling swords of the Corpse Fleet are earned based on ascension through the ranks. The reanimated ranks of the converted earn their swords through tallied kill counts, while officers receive their blades as part of the transition to the rank of commander. The blades of Corpse Fleet admirals are some of the keenest weapons in the known galaxy, despite being mostly employed as holdout weapons.

FOSSILWRAP (I–III)

Meant for first-wave boarding actions, fossilwrap armor is a cage of alchemically treated bones and steel. This armor is meant to shrug off most incoming blows while giving the wearer some amount of mobility in the thick of combat.

FRAILTY CANNON

The frailty cannon line produces a jet of necromantically fueled coolant. More easily controlled than their zero cannon counterparts, these weapons are used to bring down enemies as much as they're used to invigorate nearby undead.

FRAILTY PISTOL

A rib cage of ossified injectors covers the casing of these pistols, corrupting the internal coolant supply with negative energy. These pistols deliver chilling blasts of concentrated entropy at close range.

FRAILTY RIFLE

Standard issue to many soldiers of the Corpse Fleet, the frailty series of rifles is designed to affect only living enemies. The weapons' most common application is Corpse Fleet agents firing at enemies engaged by mindless undead, with incidents of friendly fire rewarding allies who are hit with boosts of negative energy.

NECRO GRENADE (I–IV)

These grenades are crafted to resemble leering, pygmy-sized skulls. When a necro grenade detonates, it expels a shroud of chemical coolants from its exposed eyes and mouth. This freezing gas is laced with minor traces of negative energy, draining the living and healing undead caught in the area of effect.

SKITTERHIDE (I–III)

This armor is made from the harvested hides of the remains of destroyed undead, making it resemble a macabre skinsuit. Ossified studs and embellishments reinforce the alchemically treated skin, which is otherwise designed to support Corpse Fleet agents favoring speed and stealth.

TOMB CLAW

Corpse Fleet officers directing hordes of converted covet these wicked talons. Powered by a built-in energy pack, these melee weapons resemble skeletal claws made of bone and steel. The claw weeps frost in areas with an atmosphere, and its touch freezes the skin of any living creature it strikes.

TABLE 1: BASIC MELEE WEAPONS

ONE-HANDED WEAPONS	LEVEL	PRICE	DAMAGE	CRITICAL	BULK	SPECIAL
UNCATEGORIZED						
Dueling sword, converted	4	2,100	1d8 S	–	L	Analog
Dueling sword, officer	10	18,795	3d4 S	–	L	Analog
Dueling sword, admiral	17	255,150	8d6 S	–	L	Analog

TABLE 2: ADVANCED MELEE WEAPONS

ONE-HANDED WEAPONS	LEVEL	PRICE	DAMAGE	CRITICAL	BULK	SPECIAL
CRYO						
Tomb claw, skeletal	2	777	1d4 P & C	–	1	Necrotic, powered (capacity 20, usage 1)
Tomb claw, ghoulish	7	6,510	2d4 P & C	–	1	Necrotic, powered (capacity 20, usage 1)
Tomb claw, vampiric	12	36,330	5d4 P & C	–	1	Necrotic, powered (capacity 20, usage 1)
Tomb claw, lich	16	170,100	12d4 P & C	–	1	Necrotic, powered (capacity 20, usage 1)

TABLE 3: SMALL ARMS

ONE-HANDED WEAPONS	LEVEL	PRICE	DAMAGE	RANGE	CRITICAL	CAPACITY	USAGE	BULK	SPECIAL
CRYO									
Frailty pistol, rasp-class	4	2,420	1d4 C	60 ft.	–	10 charges	1	L	Necrotic
Frailty pistol, wail-class	9	15,400	2d4 C	60 ft.	–	20 charges	2	L	Necrotic
Frailty pistol, scream-class	14	85,800	4d4 C	60 ft.	–	20 charges	2	L	Necrotic
Frailty pistol, deathcry-class	18	440,000	6d4 C	60 ft.	–	40 charges	4	L	Necrotic

TABLE 4: LONGARMS

TWO-HANDED WEAPONS	LEVEL	PRICE	DAMAGE	RANGE	CRITICAL	CAPACITY	USAGE	BULK	SPECIAL
CRYO									
Frailty rifle, atrophy-class	3	1,650	1d6 C	60 ft.	–	20 charges	2	1	Necrotic
Frailty rifle, rot-class	7	7,700	2d6 C	60 ft.	–	20 charges	2	2	Necrotic
Frailty rifle, blight-class	13	57,200	4d6 C	60 ft.	–	40 charges	4	2	Necrotic
Frailty rifle, epidemic-class	17	297,000	7d6 C	60 ft.	–	50 charges	5	2	Necrotic

TABLE 5: HEAVY WEAPONS

TWO-HANDED WEAPONS	LEVEL	PRICE	DAMAGE	RANGE	CRITICAL	CAPACITY	USAGE	BULK	SPECIAL
CRYO									
Frailty cannon, murder-class	10	20,900	3d6 C	60 ft.	–	40 charges	4	2	Line, necrotic
Frailty cannon, massacre-class	15	132,000	6d6 C	60 ft.	–	50 charges	5	2	Line, necrotic
Frailty cannon, extinction-class	19	660,000	9d6 C	80 ft.	–	50 charges	5	2	Line, necrotic

TABLE 6: GRENADES

GRENADES	LEVEL	PRICE	RANGE	CAPACITY	BULK	SPECIAL
Necro grenade I	5	870	20 ft.	Drawn	L	Explode (1d8 C, necrotic, 10 ft.)
Necro grenade II	9	3,900	20 ft.	Drawn	L	Explode (2d8 C, necrotic, 15 ft.)
Necro grenade III	13	14,640	20 ft.	Drawn	L	Explode (4d8 C, necrotic, 20 ft.)
Necro grenade IV	17	72,900	20 ft.	Drawn	L	Explode (6d8 C, necrotic, 20 ft.)

TABLE 7: LIGHT ARMOR

ARMOR MODEL	LEVEL	PRICE	EAC	KAC	MAX DEX BONUS	ARMOR CHECK PENALTY	SPEED ADJUSTMENT	UPGRADE SLOTS	BULK
Skitterhide I	3	1,200	+2	+3	+5	–	–	0	L
Skitterhide II	9	12,500	+10	+11	+7	–	–	2	L
Skitterhide III	16	144,000	+19	+19	+8	–	–	4	L

TABLE 8: HEAVY ARMOR

ARMOR MODEL	LEVEL	PRICE	EAC	KAC	MAX DEX BONUS	ARMOR CHECK PENALTY	SPEED ADJUSTMENT	UPGRADE SLOTS	BULK
Fossilwrap I	5	3,100	+9	+9	+2	-2	-5 ft.	1	2
Fossilwrap II	13	55,000	+19	+19	+4	-2	-5 ft.	5	2
Fossilwrap III	19	645,000	+25	+25	+6	-2	-5 ft.	6	2

VANGUARD OF THE CORPSE FLEET

Along with versions of the Eoxian ship styles found on pages 306–307 of the *Starfinder Core Rulebook*, the Corpse Fleet fields the following deadly vessels.

DEATH'S CURTAIN NECROFIGHTER

The Death's Curtain Necrofighter is an innovation of the Corpse Fleet's secret shipyards. A two-crew fighter, this sleek vessel is often piloted by a trained elebrian assisted by a ghoul or skeletal gunner. An integrated tactical computer—a rarity among Eoxian-designed ships—allows for the pilot to coordinate effectively with her gunner. The hull is derived from the Death's Head Necroglider (*Core Rulebook* 306), but it does not have formal ties to the Eoxian manufacturer.

DEATH'S CURTAIN NECROFIGHTER — TIER 1

Tiny fighter

Speed 12; **Maneuverability** good (turn 1)

AC 17; **TL** 16

HP 35; **DT** –; **CT** 7

Shields basic 30 (forward 10, port 7, starboard 7, aft 6)

Attack (Forward) light particle beam (3d6), light plasma torpedo launcher (3d8)

Power Core Micron Ultra (80 PCU); **Drift Engine** none; **Systems** basic short-range sensors, mk 1 duonode computer, mk 4 armor, mk 3 defenses; **Expansion Bays** none

Modifiers +1 to any two checks per round, +2 Computers; **Complement** 2 (minimum 1, maximum 2)

CREW

Gunner gunnery +5

Pilot gunnery +5, Piloting +10 (1 rank)

GRAVE CASKET

Grave Caskets are the core of Corpse Fleet military boarding and landing operations. They're almost as well armored and shielded as the Blackwind Sepulcher (*Core Rulebook* 307), but they have increased speed and room for elite commandos and squads of converted. Almost all these shuttles are equipped with an environmental chamber to accommodate living captives, since standard Corpse Fleet starships are airless.

GRAVE CASKET — TIER 3

Small shuttle

Speed 12; **Maneuverability** perfect (turn 0); **Drift** 1

AC 21; **TL** 20

HP 35; **DT** –; **CT** 7

Shields light 60 (forward 15, port 15, starboard 15, aft 15)

Attack (Forward) light plasma cannon (2d12)

Power Core Pulse Brown (90 PCU); **Drift Engine** Signal Basic; **Systems** advanced medium-range sensors, basic computer, crew quarters (common), mk 7 armor, mk 7 defenses; **Expansion Bays** cargo hold, passenger seating, sealed environmental chamber

Modifiers +4 Computers, +1 Piloting; **Complement** 4 (minimum 1, maximum 4)

CREW

Engineer Engineering +8 (3 ranks)

Gunner gunnery +8

Pilot Piloting +14 (3 ranks)

Science Officer Computers +12 (3 ranks)

PALE BUTCHER SCOUT

Pale Butcher Scouts are the solitary heralds of the Corpse Fleet, scouring Near Space and the Vast on extended missions for potential bases for Corpse Fleet activities. They also seek out bountiful harvests of living beings to be converted to mindless undead. The presence of a single Pale Butcher Scout often preludes the arrival of further Corpse Fleet vessels.

PALE BUTCHER SCOUT — TIER 4

Medium explorer

Speed 6; **Maneuverability** good (turn 1); **Drift** 2

AC 18; **TL** 17

HP 65; **DT** –; **CT** 13

Shields medium 90 (forward 25, port 20, starboard 20, aft 25)

Attack (Forward) heavy laser cannon (4d8)

Attack (Port) coilgun (4d4)

Attack (Starboard) coilgun (4d4)

Attack (Turret) high explosive missile launcher (4d8)

Power Core Arcus Heavy (130 PCU); **Drift Engine** Signal Booster; **Systems** basic computer, basic long-range sensors, crew quarters (common), mk 3 defenses, mk 4 armor; **Expansion Bays** cargo holds (2), general science lab, sealed environmental chamber

Modifiers +2 Computers , +1 Piloting ; **Complement** 6 (minimum 1, maximum 6)

CREW

Captain Bluff +10 (4 ranks), Computers +12 (4 ranks), gunnery +10, Intimidate +10 (4 ranks), Piloting +11 (4 ranks)

Engineer Engineering +15 (4 ranks)

Gunners (2) gunnery +10

Pilot Piloting +11 (4 ranks)

Science Officer Computers +12 (4 ranks)

CRYPT WARDEN

Ominous Crypt Warden destroyers form the backbone of any Corpse Fleet armada. A Crypt Warden resembles two

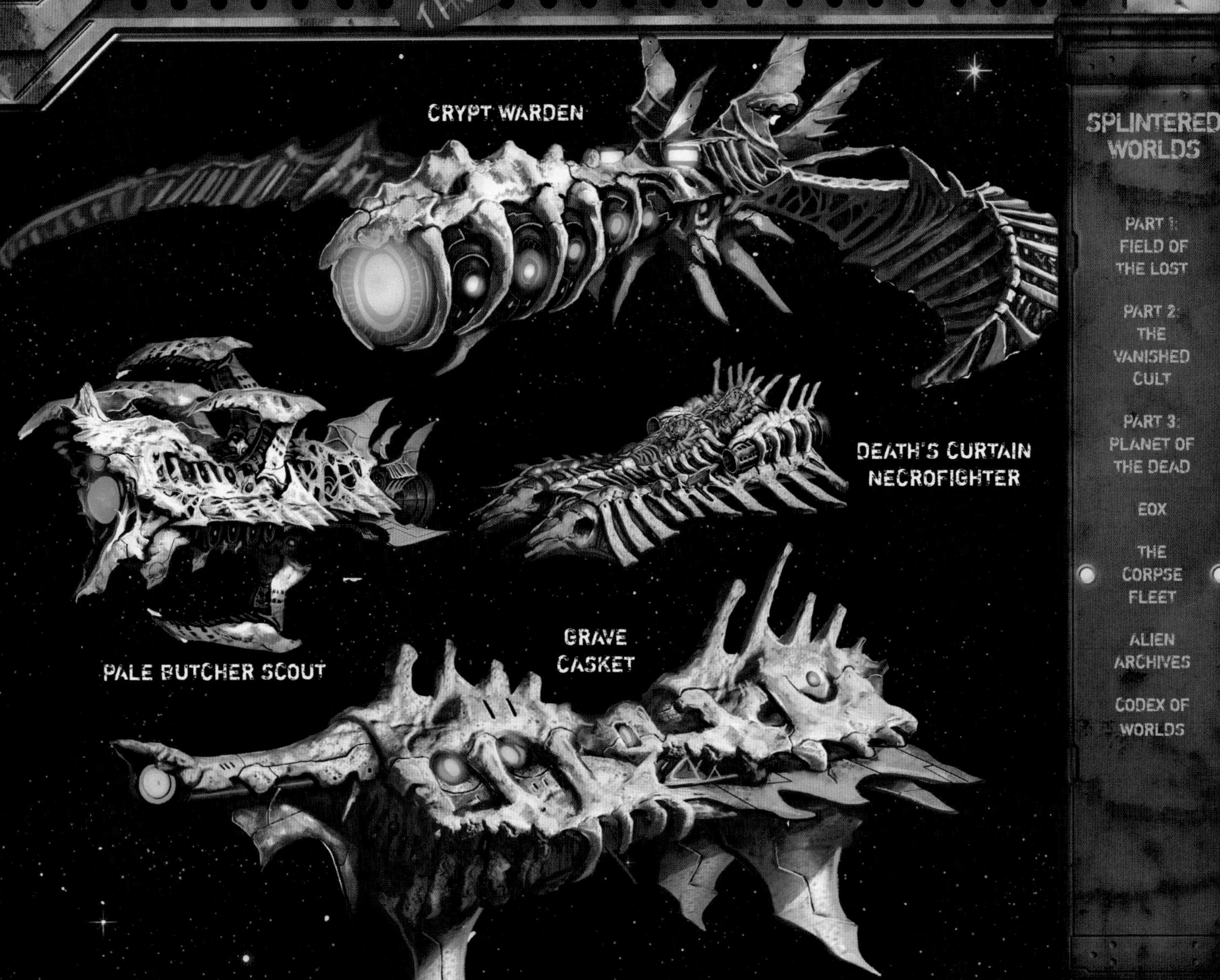

fused scythe blades made of bone, with a single powerful cannon running down the center. Made for frontal engagements, these ships intimidate enemies with their sharpened prows, shrugging off lesser attacks with their shields while returning fire with intense blasts of plasma when their EMP cannons don't immediately disable their foes. These ships are also one of the few Eoxian-designed ships to include a medical bay as a standard amenity—though the services rendered within are tailored to undead, with necromantic facilities that repair the ship's unliving crew.

CRYPT WARDEN — TIER 7

Large destroyer
Speed 6; **Maneuverability** average (turn 2); **Drift** 1
AC 21; **TL** 19
HP 170; **DT** –; **CT** 34
Shields medium 100 (forward 30, port 25, starboard 25, aft 20)
Attack (Forward) heavy laser net (5d6), plasma cannon (5d12)
Attack (Port) gyrolaser (1d8)
Attack (Starboard) gyrolaser (1d8)
Attack (Turret) light EMP cannon (special)
Power Core Arcus Maximum (200 PCU); **Drift Engine** Signal Basic; **Systems** basic computer, basic medium-range sensors, crew quarters (common), mk 4 defenses, mk 5 armor; **Expansion Bays** cargo hold, escape pods, life science lab, medical bay (modified)
Modifiers +2 Computers; **Complement** 20 (minimum 6, maximum 20)

CREW

Captain Bluff +19 (7 ranks), Computers +21 (7 ranks), gunnery +19, Intimidate +19 (7 ranks), Piloting +19 (7 ranks)
Engineer (1 officer, 6 crew) Engineering +14 (7 ranks)
Gunner (1 officer, 3 crew) gunnery +14
Pilot (1 officer, 2 crew) Piloting +14 (7 ranks)
Science Officer (1 officer, 4 crew) Computers +16 (7 ranks)

ALIEN ARCHIVES

We began the third day of our exploration of this strange new planetoid at the first light of dawn. The grunts complained again about the heat and the odd coloration of the sky, which hurt their eyes. I made Vaellis, who griped the loudest, carry part of the surveying equipment. By afternoon, the whole expedition was quiet… as was the surrounding landscape. Dr. Sixx noted that she hadn't heard the sounds of any wildlife for the past few miles. That's when the lizard-thing crawled from a nearby ravine, black mist pouring from its eyes. The three closest to it—Dzeski, Hou, and Meiruda—pulled their guns and started shooting… at each other, while Dr. Sixx—one of the sharpest minds in the galaxy—simply stood there and recited a mixture of poetry and mathematical formulae. I called for a retreat while Vaellis dropped a smoke grenade. I lost two of my soldiers in the ensuing mess, but the rest of us made it back to our previous camp. I now understand why no one has colonized this godsforsaken rock yet.

—From the personal log of Captain Lyoso Bexigen
of the Exo-Angels mercenary squad

ELEBRIAN

CR 1/3 XP 135

N Medium humanoid (elebrian)
Init +1; **Senses** low-light vision; **Perception** –1

DEFENSE **HP** 6
EAC 11; **KAC** 12
Fort +0; **Ref** +2; **Will** +2

OFFENSE
Speed 30 ft.
Melee tactical baton +0 (1d4 B)
Ranged azimuth laser pistol +2 (1d4 F; critical burn 1d4)
Offensive Abilities find weakness

STATISTICS
Str +0; **Dex** +1; **Con** +1; **Int** +3; **Wis** –1; **Cha** +0
Skills Computers +3, Culture +3, Engineering +7, Life Science +3, Mysticism +7, Physical Science +7
Languages Akitonian, Castrovelian, Common, Eoxian
Gear estex suit I, azimuth laser pistol with 2 batteries (20 charges each), tactical baton
Other Abilities intellectual knack

SPECIAL ABILITIES
Find Weakness (Ex) Elebrians can instinctively find and take advantage of other creatures' weak points. An elebrian can make a single melee or ranged attack as a full action, and if she hits, she can add half her level to the damage dealt (minimum +1 damage). Whether successful or not, once an elebrian has used this ability on a creature, that creature is immune to it for 24 hours.
Intellectual Knack (Ex) Elebrians can easily comprehend complex issues and remember minutia. An elebrian can attempt a skill check to recall knowledge untrained, regardless of the DC, and can always take 20 to do so (though this takes 2 minutes), even without access to an information network or data set.

RACIAL TRAITS

Ability Adjustments: +2 Con, +2 Int, –2 Wis
Hit Points: 2

Size and Type: Elebrians are Medium humanoids with the elebrian subtype.
Find Weakness: See the stat block.
Intellectual Knack: See the stat block.
Low-Light Vision: Elebrians can see in dim light as if it were normal light.

Elebrians, the native race of Eox, were nearly wiped out in the calamity that ravaged the planet. Only a tiny population of living elebrians now remain.

Elebrians are very humanlike, and it has been suggested that they and humanity may share a common ancestor in the ancient past. A typical elebrian stands slightly over 6 feet tall and has pale skin and large, dark eyes. They have oversized craniums with slightly distended foreheads to house their large brains. Most elebrians are entirely hairless, but a small minority grow wispy hair on their scalps and thin eyebrows.

Elebrians have quick wits and a natural desire to accumulate both knowledge and power. They are driven to undertake tasks that provide either a valued insight or a significant personal advantage.

GHOUL CR 1 XP 400

CE Medium undead

Init +4; **Senses** darkvision 60 ft.; **Perception** +10

DEFENSE **HP** 18

EAC 14; **KAC** 14

Fort +3; **Ref** +3; **Will** +3

Immunities undead immunities

OFFENSE

Speed 30 ft.

Melee bite +5 (1d6+3 P plus ghoul fever and paralysis) or claw +5 (1d6+3 S plus paralysis)

Ranged azimuth laser pistol +8 (1d4+1 F; critical burn 1d4)

STATISTICS

Str +2; **Dex** +4; **Con** –; **Int** +1; **Wis** +0; **Cha** +1

Skills Acrobatics +5, Athletics +5, Stealth +10

Languages Common, Eoxian

Other Abilities unliving

Gear azimuth laser pistol with 1 battery (20 charges)

ECOLOGY

Environment any

Organization solitary, gang (2–6), or pack (7–12)

SPECIAL ABILITIES

Paralysis (Ex) When a ghoul deals damage to a creature with its bite or claw attack, the target must succeed at a DC 12 Fortitude saving throw or gain the paralyzed condition for 1d4+1 rounds. As a full action, the target can attempt a new saving throw to end the condition. Elves are immune to this ability.

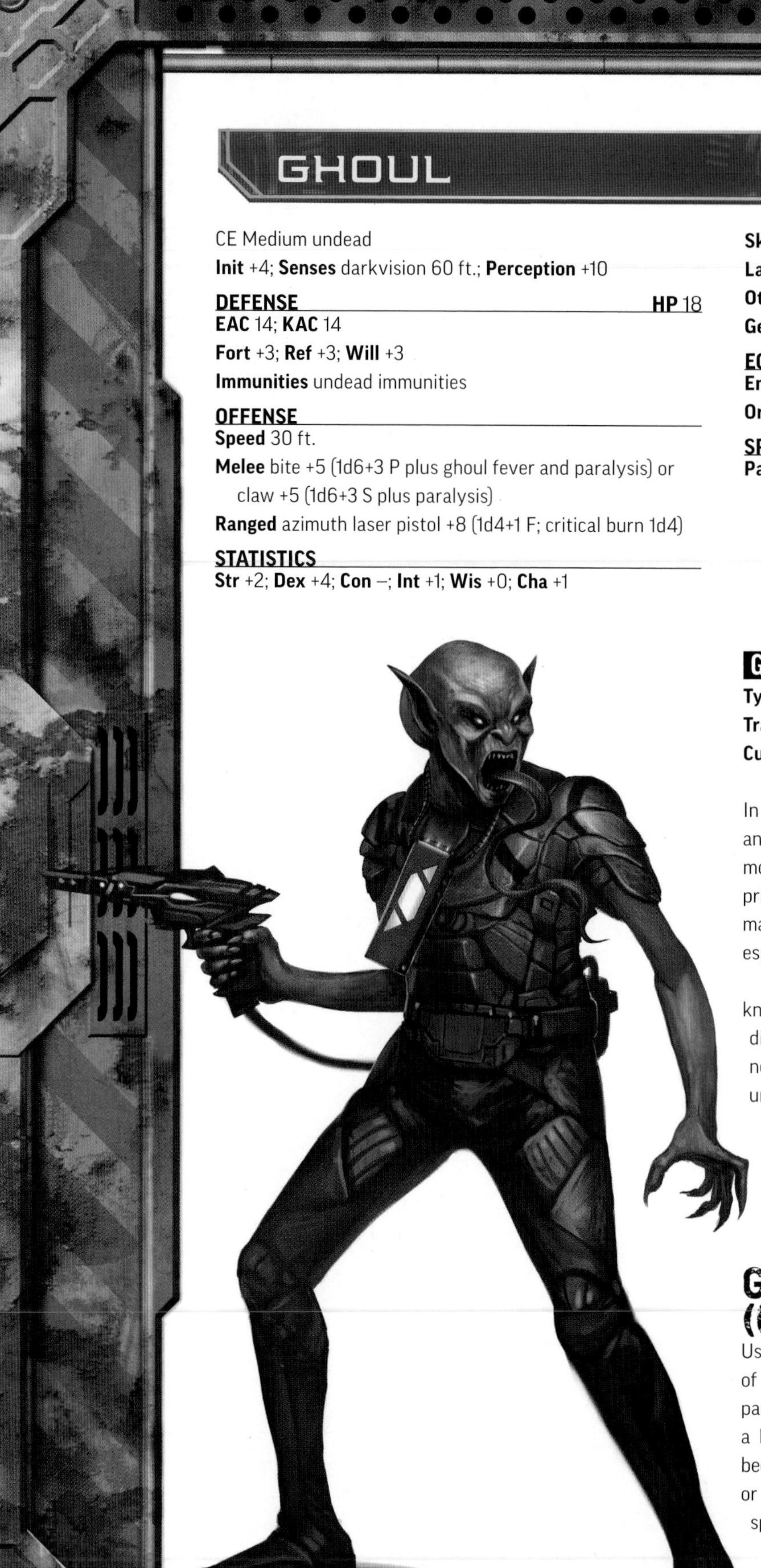

GHOUL FEVER

Type disease (injury); **Save** Fortitude DC 12

Track physical; **Frequency** 1/day

Cure 1 save

In ages past, ghouls shunned society and haunted cemeteries and city sewers. However, ghouls in the Pact Worlds are often more likely to live in cities, especially settlements inhabited primarily by undead. Ghouls are resourceful and hardy, and make good workers across a variety of industries. Ghouls are especially populous on the undead planet of Eox.

Ghouls spread—sometimes purposefully—a virulent disease known as ghoul fever through their saliva. A creature that dies of ghoul fever often rises as a ghoul within 24 hours; if not checked immediately, ghoul fever can quickly lead to an undead population explosion.

Certain powerful ghouls known as ghasts can affect even elves with their paralysis and exude a powerful stench; these undead usually hold important positions in ghoul society. Ghouls that lurk underwater and in coastal areas are called lacedons.

GHOUL TEMPLATE GRAFT (CR 1/2+)

Use the following template graft to create a unique ghoul of any CR. A ghast has a stench aura out to 10 feet and its paralysis ability can affect elves. A target must succeed at a Fortitude saving throw when entering a ghast's aura or becomes sickened for 1d6+4 minutes. Ghasts should be CR 3 or higher. A lacedon gains the aquatic subtype and a swim speed of 30 feet.

Required Creature Type: Undead.

Suggested Array: Combatant or expert.

Abilities: Bite attack that inflicts ghoul fever and paralysis; claw attack that inflicts paralysis.

Suggested Ability Modifiers: Dexterity, Strength.

MARROWBLIGHT

CR 7 **XP 3,200**

CE Medium undead
Init +4; **Senses** darkvision 60 ft.; **Perception** +14

DEFENSE **HP** 105
EAC 19; **KAC** 21
Fort +9; **Ref** +9; **Will** +8
Immunities undead immunities

OFFENSE
Speed 30 ft.
Melee claw +17 (1d8+12 S) or
spur +17 (1d8+12 P plus red ache)
Multiattack claw +12 (1d8+12), spur +12 (1d8+12 plus red ache)
Offensive Abilities pounce

STATISTICS
Str +5; **Dex** +4; **Con** –; **Int** +2; **Wis** +1; **Cha** –1
Skills Acrobatics +14, Athletics +14, Intimidate +19
Languages Common, Eoxian
Other Abilities unliving

ECOLOGY
Environment any ruins (Eox)
Organization solitary

SPECIAL ABILITIES
Pounce (Ex) As a standard action, a marrowblight can leap up to 15 feet into an empty space, provoking attacks of opportunity as normal for this movement. Each creature in a square adjacent to the marrowblight at the end of its movement must succeed at a DC 15 Reflex saving throw or gain the off-target condition for 1 round. Creatures that fail this check by 10 or more are also knocked prone. The marrowblight can exclude a number of allies from this effect equal to its Intelligence modifier (2 for most marrowblights).

Marrowblights are muscular undead monstrosities filled with hate. They typically arise from brawny humanoids that were exposed to strange radiation or arcane energy that painfully warped their flesh at the moments of demise, creating hideous bone spurs that protrude from the creatures' backs, cheeks, jaws, and shoulders. Marrowblights can use these spurs as weapons, as they drip with the disease that courses through the creature's undead bones like marrow.

Scientifically advanced planets, such as Eox in the Pact Worlds, have pinpointed the biology-warping processes required to create marrowblights, and some elebrians have willingly succumbed to this horrific undead fate. On Eox, naturally occurring marrowblights created during the planet's cataclysm still exist. These are typically among the universe's most vicious and hateful undead, eschewing society and living creatures in particular. Sometimes, though, such marrowblights ally with forces that seek to assert and spread the superiority of undead creatures throughout the universe and beyond, including the Corpse Fleet and those who sympathize with the exiled navy.

Marrowblights are typically 8 to 10 feet tall—including the horrific bone spurs that protrude from their backs—and weigh upward of 300 pounds.

MARROWBLIGHT TEMPLATE GRAFT (CR 5+)

Use the following template graft to create a unique marrowblight of any CR.

Required Creature Type: Undead.

Suggested Array: Combatant.

Traits: Spur attack that causes disease (Fortitude save should be appropriate for CR); pounce.

Suggested Ability Modifiers: Strength, Constitution.

SKREELING

CR 3 **XP** 800

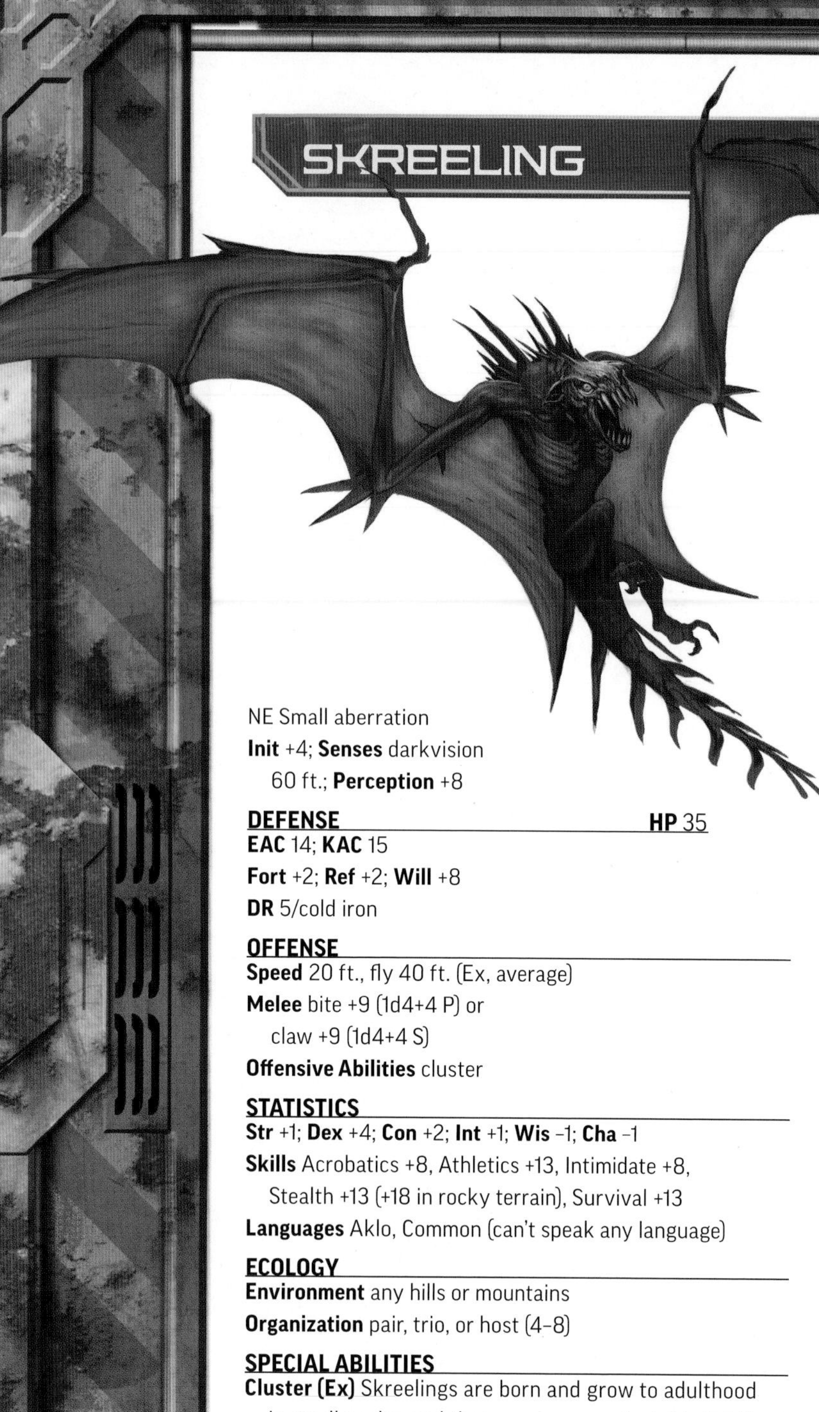

Brutal and shrewd, skreelings are the immature offspring of skreesires (see page 57), but they have not yet developed the full mental abilities of their progenitors. Skreeling siblings hunt in packs, pooling their nascent fighting abilities, and they are much stronger when they work together. Skreeling hosts, as xenobiologists call these packs, often live in rocky crannies or caves where they can better protect themselves from threats until they reach adulthood. Although they lack telepathy and the physical characteristics that would allow them to speak, skreelings can emit shrill, distinctive battle cries, often to distract prey or frighten predators away from their lairs.

Skreelings are typically found on rocky planetoids with thin atmospheres, and they almost always lair within 100 yards or so of a parent skreesire's territory. Skreelings hatch from eggs their parent has laid in corpses, gathered brush, or nests of sand; they then work together to survive until they reach adulthood. Skreelings are omnivorous and even ingest ash, metal shavings, or wood when regular food is scarce. Once the vicious creatures reach adulthood, their expanded intellects combined with their burgeoning appetites for territory often see siblings turn on each other until the host eventually disperses and the individual skreelings search for new lairs.

Skreelings typically stand about 3 feet tall, weigh about 30 pounds, and have a wingspan of about 3-1/2 feet—although, as the creatures grow larger, their wings lose their functionality, their lower legs atrophy and drop off, and their tails develop into multiple ambulatory tentacles. This is a very gradual process that begins the moment they are born.

Occasionally, a skreeling becomes stunted in its development, growing too large to fly but not yet having a skreesire's psychic faculties. These mutants—known as "skreemules"—are often killed by their siblings, but they sometimes escape to live miserable solitary lives, crawling through the hills on their malformed tentacles and snapping at any potential prey.

Though uncommon, skreeling infestations near civilized settlements are treated more like natural hazards to be avoided than pests to be eliminated. Some residents even derive a kind of pride from these annoyances, going so far as to name geological features of the area or local businesses after the creatures. These citizens make sure to warn travelers and newcomers about the skreeling lairs, as much to keep the flying aberrations safe as the people they caution. However, they are quick to turn on the skreelings if they get too aggressive and hold no such love for their far more dangerous adult forms.

NE Small aberration
Init +4; **Senses** darkvision 60 ft.; **Perception** +8

DEFENSE **HP** 35
EAC 14; **KAC** 15
Fort +2; **Ref** +2; **Will** +8
DR 5/cold iron

OFFENSE
Speed 20 ft., fly 40 ft. (Ex, average)
Melee bite +9 (1d4+4 P) or claw +9 (1d4+4 S)
Offensive Abilities cluster

STATISTICS
Str +1; **Dex** +4; **Con** +2; **Int** +1; **Wis** –1; **Cha** –1
Skills Acrobatics +8, Athletics +13, Intimidate +8, Stealth +13 (+18 in rocky terrain), Survival +13
Languages Aklo, Common (can't speak any language)

ECOLOGY
Environment any hills or mountains
Organization pair, trio, or host (4–8)

SPECIAL ABILITIES
Cluster (Ex) Skreelings are born and grow to adulthood in small packs, and they are more comfortable fighting alongside other skreelings, including their siblings. When two or more skreelings flank a single creature, each skreeling attacking that creature receives an additional +1 circumstance bonus to attack rolls. When two or more skreelings flank a single creature, each skreeling deals 1 point of bleed damage in addition to its normal damage on a successful hit. This bleed damage stacks with bleed damage from other skreelings, but not with itself. (For instance, two skreelings that flank a single creature each deal 1 point of bleed damage every round that they successfully attack, but each individual skreeling can never deal more than 1 bleed damage per round.)

SKREESIRE

CR 7 **XP** 3,200

NE Large aberration

Init +4; **Senses** darkvision 60 ft.; **Perception** +14

DEFENSE **HP** 100

EAC 19; **KAC** 20

Fort +6; **Ref** +6; **Will** +12

DR 5/cold iron; **Immunities** acid

OFFENSE

Speed 30 ft., swim 20 ft.

Melee bite +15 (1d8+9 P) or tentacle +15 (1d8+9 B plus grab)

Space 10 ft.; **Reach** 10 ft.

Offensive Abilities enthrall

STATISTICS

Str +2; **Dex** +4; **Con** +1; **Int** +5; **Wis** +1; **Cha** –2

Skills Acrobatics +14, Athletics +19, Intimidate +14, Stealth +19 (+24 in rocky terrain), Survival +19

Languages Aklo, Common (can't speak any language); telepathy 100 ft.

Other Abilities camouflage

ECOLOGY

Environment any hills or mountains

Organization solitary

SPECIAL ABILITIES

Camouflage (Ex) Skreesires have a mottled exterior that blends in well with their preferred surroundings in rocky hill and mountain terrains. In addition to a skreesire's normal racial bonus to Stealth, when a skreesire remains stationary for 1 round in rocky terrain, it gains a +10 circumstance bonus to Stealth checks (this bonus doesn't stack with the *invisibility* spell or similar effects). If the skreesire takes any action, it loses this bonus until it once again spends 1 round remaining stationary.

Enthrall (Su) Skreesires have powerful wills and can use them to change the course of an intelligent creature's thoughts. Three times per day as a standard action, a skreesire can project its will into the mind of an intelligent creature with 40 feet. The target hears a mighty telepathic screech, and if it fails a DC 17 Will saving throw, it is affected as per *suggestion*. Whether or not it succeeds at its save, a creature can't be affected by the same skreesire's enthrall ability for 24 hours. This is a mind-affecting effect.

Skreesires are insidious horrors that lurk in the rocky reaches of the universe. They are omnivorous and consume all manner of matter, but they prefer the same diet of plants that sustains and empowers their progeny—nasty winged creatures known as skreelings (see page 56). Skreesires round bodies are bulky and intimidating. Their wings are nonfunctional, and they use their tentacles for grabbing prey. They stand up to 10 feet tall and weigh up to 500 pounds.

Unlike their young, skreesires live solitary lives and are fiercely protective of their territories, even from other skreesires. They view any intrusion from a sentient creature as a threat, and thus they often use their infamous mental abilities to twist intruders' minds and cause those creatures to flee. If that fails, they descend on the trespasser with teeth and tentacles.

Skreesires are hermaphroditic and can self-fertilize, though they usually do so only after particularly large feasts, as extra genetic material they harvest from their food helps to mitigate the effects of inbreeding. They tend to lay their clutches of eggs in the corpses of the creatures they have just fed upon, but they use soft sand or tangles of vines if needed.

VAMPIRE, JIANG-SHI

CR 6 **XP** 2,400

Elebrian jiang-shi operative
LE Medium undead
Init +6; **Senses** blindsight (breath) 60 ft., darkvision 60 ft.; **Perception** +19

DEFENSE **HP** 80

EAC 18; **KAC** 20
Fort +5, **Ref** +8, **Will** +9
Defensive Abilities evasion, fast healing 5, prayer scroll; **DR** 10/magic; **Immunities** effects from spell gems, undead immunities; **Resistances** cold 10
Weaknesses jiang-shi weaknesses

OFFENSE

Speed 30 ft.
Melee bite +12 (1d6+8 P) or claw +14 (1d6+8 S plus grab)
Ranged advanced shirren-eye rifle +14 (2d10+6 P) or corona laser pistol +14 (2d4+6 F; critical burn 1d4)
Offensive Abilities debilitating trick, deft claws, drain chi, trick attack +3d8

STATISTICS

Str +2, **Dex** +5, **Con** –, **Int** +3, **Wis** +3, **Cha** +2
Skills Acrobatics +19, Bluff +19, Disguise +19, Engineering +14, Stealth +14
Languages Common, Eoxian
Other Abilities hopping gait, operative exploits (debilitating sniper, master of disguise [2/day, 60 minutes or 6 minutes, DC 16]), specialization (spy), unliving
Gear freebooter armor II, advanced shirren-eye rifle with 25 sniper rounds, corona laser pistol with 2 batteries (20 charges each)

ECOLOGY

Environment any
Organization solitary or cabal (2–8)

SPECIAL ABILITIES

Blindsight (Ex) A jiang-shi can sense the breathing of living creatures. A creature that holds its breath or doesn't need to breathe cannot be perceived by a jiang-shi's blindsight.

Deft Claws (Ex) A jiang-shi's claw attack has the grab ability (*Starfinder Alien Archive* 155) and the operative weapon special property.

Drain Chi (Su) When a jiang-shi succeeds at a grapple combat maneuver, it can drain "chi," or life energy, by drinking its victim's breath. A victim must succeed at DC 16 Fortitude save or gain 1 negative level and be staggered for 1d4 rounds.

Hopping Gait (Ex) A jiang-shi moves by hopping, and its land speed is reduced by 10 feet from its base creature's speed (this adjustment is already included in the statistics above). A jiang-shi ignores difficult terrain and can't be tripped. Other speeds (such as fly and swim speeds) are unaffected by this ability.

Jiang-Shi Weaknesses (Ex) A jiang-shi is held at bay by cooked rice, mirrors, or ringing a handbell. It must stay at least 5 feet away from the object of its revulsion and cannot touch or make melee attacks against a creature brandishing such an object. Holding a jiang-shi at bay is a standard action. After being held at bay for 1 round, a jiang-shi can attempt a DC 20 Will save at the beginning of its turn to act normally.

Prayer Scroll (Su) The holographic prayer scroll at a jiang-shi's brow grants immunity to any effects from spell gems or other items that store spells, as if the jiang-shi had unbeatable spell resistance. It also grants the jiang-shi fast healing 5 and prevents the jiang-shi from being destroyed. When reduced to 0 Hit Points, a jiang-shi crumbles to dust, but it re-forms in 1 minute with 1 Hit Point in the nearest unoccupied space. Scattering the dust or mixing rice into the dust with a dose of vinegar before the jiang-shi re-forms destroys it permanently.

Jiang-shis (often called "hopping vampires") are grotesque undead creatures that drink the breath of the living to feed on their life energy, or "chi." A creature can become a jiang-shi when its spirit does not depart when the creature dies, instead remaining within the rotting corpse. Eventually, the decomposing body reanimates and the newly risen jiang-shi goes in search of living creatures to feed upon.

A jiang-shi's appearance depends on both the circumstances of the creature's death and the state of its corpse at the time of its reanimation. A jiang-shi that fell to its death on a warm, wet world would likely have twisted or broken limbs and be in a state of advanced putrefaction, while one who was killed by laser fire on an airless asteroid in the void of space might exhibit laser burns but manifest no signs of decomposition at all. Regardless of the state of decay, most jiang-shis wear clothing or gear that is out of style, if not completely outdated, due to the fact that it can take decades—or even centuries—before a jiang-shi rises from the dead.

All jiang-shis display a prayer scroll in front of their faces. In ancient, pre-Gap days, these prayer scrolls were handwritten on parchment and affixed to the corpse's brow with stitches or staples in order to protect the deceased from the ravages of restless spirits. In modern times, holographic prayer scrolls projected in front of a jiang-shi's forehead have typically replaced the parchment scrolls and protect the jiang-shi's body from both physical and magical harm. If a jiang-shi's prayer scroll is ever stolen or destroyed, it loses the defensive benefits granted by the scroll (see above), but the jiang-shi may replace it with a handwritten scroll. This requires a strip of paper or cloth, a writing implement, and 10 minutes of uninterrupted work. Alternatively, a jiang-shi can recreate a holographic prayer scroll by crafting a hybrid holoskin (*Starfinder Core Rulebook* 220) to project the scroll. This requires at least 2 ranks in both the Engineering and Mysticism skills and UPBs worth 500 credits.

Because most jiang-shis become undead only after their corpses have undergone some measure of decomposition, their bodies often display signs of rigor mortis. The rigid inflexibility of a jiang-shi's muscle tissue makes the creature's movements especially stiff, and causes the distinctive bouncing gait which gives jiang-shis their colloquial name of hopping vampires. Nevertheless, jiang-shis can be surprisingly nimble in rough terrain, and the stiffness of their joints has little adverse effect in zero gravity.

Jiang-shis are horrified by their own reflections, and the sound of a handbell or the call of a rooster fills them with terror. Cooked rice, which reminds jiang-shis that they are dead and can no longer eat normal food, shames them. Curiously, uncooked rice and other types of grain (cooked or not) don't affect jiang-shis at all, though rice mixed with vinegar and the dust of a destroyed jiang-shi prevents that vampire from returning to unlife.

Although they normally try to avoid daylight, jiang-shis suffer no detrimental effects from sunlight and can move around during the day unharmed. Nevertheless, most jiang-shis prefer to operate at night or in darkness, when their more obvious physical traits are not as noticeable to the living among whom they mingle. On the other hand, a glowing holographic prayer scroll can be difficult to conceal in the darkness.

Jiang-shis tend to lead solitary existences, but they are not averse to working with other undead creatures, especially if those undead feed on the flesh of the living, leaving the victim's chi for the jiang-shi to drain. However, jiang-shis are known to be jealous of blood-sucking vampires because of their ability to create their own undead spawn. As a result, most hopping vampires refuse to cooperate with their bloodsucking rivals, even if they might profit from such an arrangement.

In the Pact Worlds, jiang-shis are most associated with the dead world of Eox, though the hopping vampires can be found anywhere there are living, breathing creatures to feed upon. Some jiang-shis serve as officers in the exiled Corpse Fleet as well, working just as tirelessly as their other undead comrades-in-arms for Eoxian supremacy and independence. At least one of the Golden League's powerful families is said to be led by an ancient jiang-shi matriarch who was alive on pre-Gap Golarion, and inhabitants of Absalom Station's "Downside" swear that a cabal of seven jiang-shis has inhabited an abandoned level of the Spike since at least the end of the Gap. Each member of the cabal supposedly "specializes" in drinking the breath of just one species, and refuses to feed on the chi of a different race.

JIANG-SHI VAMPIRE TEMPLATE GRAFT (CR 5+)

When a restless spirit does not leave its corpse at the time of death and instead festers and putrefies within its decomposing mortal shell, it can eventually rise as an undead jiang-shi vampire.

Required Creature Type: Undead.

Suggested Array: Any.

Traits: Blindsight (breath) 60 ft.; DR 10/magic; cold resistance 10; jiang-shi weaknesses.

Abilities: Deft claws, drain chi, hopping gait, prayer scroll.

Suggested Ability Score Modifiers: Dexterity, Wisdom.

VEOLISK

CR 6 XP 2,400

CE Medium magical beast
Init +6; **Senses** darkvision 60 ft., low-light vision; **Perception** +13

DEFENSE **HP** 90

EAC 18; **KAC** 20
Fort +10; **Ref** +10; **Will** +5

OFFENSE

Speed 20 ft.
Melee bite +17 (1d8+11 P)
Offensive Abilities void gaze (30 ft., DC 16)

STATISTICS

Str +5; **Dex** +2; **Con** +3; **Int** –4; **Wis** +0; **Cha** +2
Skills Acrobatics +13, Intimidate +13, Stealth +18

ECOLOGY

Environment any
Organization solitary or pair

SPECIAL ABILITIES

Void Gaze (Ex) A veolisk embodies the claustrophobic, dark, and often maddening aspects of deep space, and it can project a sliver of the void into its enemies with its mere gaze. A creature that fails a DC 16 Will saving throw against this gaze ability is confused until the beginning of its next turn. This is a mind-affecting effect.

Veolisks are lumbering, reptilelike quadrupeds with bony exoskeletons. They are often compared to many planets' prehistoric megafauna, despite being much smaller. Veolisks are typically found only on remote planets and planetoids in the Vast, as most xenobiologists believe their maddening gazes tend to drive off other species and make settling near veolisk territory very difficult. If veolisks are discovered near established communities, the creatures are usually hunted ruthlessly until there are none left.

The veolisk's signature void gaze ability has led to speculation that the creatures are descended from ancestors with similar gaze attacks that had far more severe effects, and they have earned the nickname "void basilisks" from those versed in the ancient folklore of Golarion. Some sages believe destruction-loving cultists of the Devourer bred the first veolisks millennia ago, well before the Gap. Whether or not this is true, the beasts have become popular as guardians of remote Devourer cult bases and as pets to those who believe themselves to be at one with the universe's entropy. Curiously, though most cultures would never think to try domesticating veolisks, the beasts become quite docile and mostly harmless when wearing blinders, veils, or other methods of negating their gaze ability.

These hulking beasts can survive on very little food, usually eating only one small meal—flesh, fruits, fungus, plant life, or anything it can find—a day. Scientists don't agree on exactly what maintains a veolisk's physiology; some believe the creatures simply have a hyperefficient metabolism, while others suggest that they feed on cosmic radiation like trees gathering sustenance through photosynthesis. A few experts theorize that veolisks don't need to eat at all to survive and subsist solely on the background arcane energies that are present everywhere in the galaxy. Reputable xenobiologists tend to scoff at this hypothesis, but their opponents are quick to point out that universe is full of strange and unknowable wonders that defy scientific explanation.

Veolisks lay fist-sized leathery eggs, usually six to eight at a time. These eggs are recognizable as belonging to a veolisk due to their ebony coloring and their tendency to give off faint wisps of odorless smoke. Once laid, the eggs don't require any kind of incubation and usually hatch on their own after a few weeks. In most broods, the first veolisks to hatch tend to devour the unhatched eggs as their first meals. Veolisk young begin to hunt for themselves after this initial meal and are fully mature in less than a year. Adult veolisks usually mate whenever the opportunity presents itself, though neither parent takes any interest in their eggs or offspring.

A typical veolisk is about 7 feet long from the tip of its snout to the end of its tail and weighs approximately 200 pounds.

BARROW

Corpse Fleet spacedock
Diameter: ×1; **Mass:** ×1
Gravity: ×1
Location: The Vast
Atmosphere: None
Day: –; **Year:** –

Untold millennia ago, an unnamed planet was pulled from its regular orbit and launched into the greater galaxy. If any life existed on this world, it died long ago, leaving the planet a barren, airless rock hurtling aimlessly through the void. Shortly after the advent of Drift travel, scouts of the Eoxian Navy discovered the rogue planet during a routine reconnaissance mission. The bone sages marked the dark world as a possible site for a future colony, but these plans were forgotten only a few years later when Eox signed the Absalom Pact and the Corpse Fleet abandoned its home world.

A few decades ago, however, an enterprising Corpse Fleet navigator stumbled across records of the rogue planet's existence. In need of a place to repair its vessels and build new ones, the Corpse Fleet established a base on the forgotten world, which its new occupiers named Barrow. With no rotation and no sun to orbit, Barrow has no days or years, and as the planet is constantly on the move, Corpse Fleet command doesn't see the need to dismantle it like it has for many other production facilities. Barrow hosts a massive shipbuilding facility that is perhaps the largest producer of Corpse Fleet vessels. On the rare occasions when Barrow passes close to a viable target, the Corpse Fleet uses the planet to devastating effect, launching dozens of fighters directly from the base without the need of carriers or transports.

Recently, top Corpse Fleet scientists completed an audacious plan: by attaching massive thrusters and Drift engines to certain parts of Barrow, they hoped to direct the rogue planet's flight, possibly even engaging in interstellar travel. The resulting explosive catastrophe destroyed most of the personnel involved and shattered part of the planet. A continent-sized chunk of Barrow now floats a few hundred meters from its previous location, though it is held in place—for now—by the remaining planet's gravitational pull. This region, dubbed "the Fracture" by Corpse Fleet grunts, still contains remnants of the failed experiment, as well as several strange entities that seem to phase in and out of reality. These creatures seem mostly harmless, despite their grotesque appearances, but when several of them manifest at once, they begin to drain the necromantic energy that animates the Corpse Fleet's undead soldiers. As a result, the Fracture has been marked as off-limits.

Since the disaster, a seasoned necrovite Corpse Fleet officer named Commodore Knarstov has taken command of the base. She has enacted strict guidelines curtailing the work of the resident scientists and technicians in order to avoid a mistake similar to that which resulted in the downfall of her predecessor, and she is determined to exceed the yearly quota for building new vessels imposed by Corpse Fleet high command. Luckily, Knarstov doesn't have to worry about the comfort or morale of her troops and appears to be well on her way to achieving her goals. Commodore Knarstov knows her job isn't a glamorous one, but she doesn't care much about personal glory, focusing only on keeping the Corpse Fleet strong and ready to face any enemy.

NEXT MONTH

THE RUINED CLOUDS

By Jason Keeley

Still on the heels of the Devourer cult, the heroes head to a distant, uncharted star system, where they find the ruins of an ancient alien city floating in the atmosphere of a gas giant. Exploring the ruins, they encounter the degenerate descendants of a highly advanced species that once controlled the alien superweapon the heroes are searching for. Through the legends and superstitions of these savage aliens, the heroes can piece together clues to the superweapon's hidden location and the key to unlocking its power—an impossibly huge megastructure that the Cult of the Devourer is intent on seizing!

ISTAMAK

By Jason Keeley

Once a vibrant metropolis and important colony of an ancient alien civilization, Istamak is now home to a tribe of technologically backward descendants of the city's original citizens. With flora and fauna now running wild amid skyscrapers and factories, the inhabitants must fight for survival as they worship the accomplishments of their ancestors. Explore Istamak's many notable locations, from overgrown parks to dilapidated theaters, and discover the equipment the current dwellers forged from the ruins of their forebears' society.

ALLUVION AND THE DRIFT

By Joe Pasini

The Drift was a gift from Triune, the god of artificial intelligence and computers, which acts as a transitory dimension making interstellar travel possible. Learn about this mysterious plane and visit Alluvion, the strange city that is Triune's home within the Drift!

MAKE YOUR GAME OUT OF THIS WORLD!

ENHANCE YOUR STARFINDER CAMPAIGNS WITH THESE EXCITING ACCESSORIES!

The *Starfinder Core Rulebook* has all the rules you need to play the game, but there are still light years of new territory to explore! Let the veteran authors of the first Starfinder Adventure Path surprise you with the twists and turns of an entire Starfinder campaign, and bring your game to life on the table with a gorgeous GM screen and hundreds of character pawns designed specifically for Starfinder's brand of science fantasy. However you play, Paizo has products to help you streamline your game and immerse yourself in a universe full of weird worlds and unique aliens. After all, when the stars are your destination, you can never be too prepared!

STARFINDER GM SCREEN

Protect your important notes and die rolls from players' prying eyes with the *Starfinder GM Screen*! This beautiful four-panel screen features stunning artwork of a breathtaking battle scene on the players' side and a huge number of helpful tables and information on the GM's side to speed up play and keep key rules at your fingertips.

$19.99 • PZO7102 • ISBN 978-1-60125-957-8

STARFINDER CORE RULEBOOK PAWN COLLECTION

The friends and foes from the Starfinder Roleplaying Game have landed in the *Starfinder Core Rulebook Pawn Collection*, which features a horde of pawns for use with the Starfinder Roleplaying Game, the Pathfinder Roleplaying Game, or any tabletop RPG! What's more, the set also contains over a dozen different starship pawns designed for use with Starfinder's starship combat system! Printed on sturdy cardstock, each double-sided pawn presents a beautiful full-color image of a character or creature drawn from the *Starfinder Core Rulebook* and the *Starfinder: First Contact* free preview bestiary. These pawns are perfect for representing both player characters and their fearsome opponents.

$24.99 • PZO7402 • ISBN 978-1-60125-960-8

STARFINDER ALIEN ARCHIVE PAWN BOX

The invasion begins with this horde of alien creatures both friendly and fearsome! The *Starfinder Alien Archive Pawn Box* presents beautiful full-color images of all the strange creatures from the *Starfinder Alien Archive*, usable as both foes and player characters. Double-sided and printed on sturdy cardstock, these are perfect for use with the Starfinder Roleplaying Game or any tabletop RPG! Each cardstock pawn comes labeled for easy sorting and slots into a size-appropriate plastic base, making the pawns easy to mix with traditional metal or plastic miniatures. With multiple pawns for commonly encountered foes and nearly 250 distinct creature images, the *Starfinder Alien Archive Pawn Box* has exactly what you need to bring the game's most popular monsters to life!

$44.99 • PZO7403 • ISBN 978-1-60125-994-3